The MIDWIFE

Companion

The art of support during birth

Andrea Robertson

ACE Graphics

Published by ACE Graphics
PO Box 366
Camperdown NSW 2050
Australia
Phone: +61 (02) 9660 5177
Fax: +61 (02) 9660 5147

First published 1997
Reprinted 2000

ISBN 0 9588015 3 3

Printed in Australia by Australian Print Group
Cover design by John Lee
Illustrations by Helen Brawley and Joanne Acty
Text design and layout by James Robertson

Body text is 10 point Palatino, headings are Zapf Humanist.

FOREWORD

When I was training to be a midwife, I sat through many lectures and read many books on the skills required for being a midwife. I sat at the feet of many midwives in clinical practice and learned as much as I could from them. When I qualified I believed that I had been given all the skills I would need as a midwife.

The real world proved rather different. Although before I started my training I had the benefit of many years of working with pregnant women through my teaching with the National Childbirth Trust, I discovered that as a midwife I was being asked to deal with women who came in all shapes and sizes, and with a bewildering array of personal needs. These were not the neat archetypes of midwifery textbooks, but living, breathing people who looked to me for guidance and support. I began to see that my formal training was only a foundation, and my real education was only just beginning.

In fact, it has been the women who have taught me all that I know about the real art of midwifery. They have been the ones who forced me to manage their twins and breech babies safely, and who encouraged me to take the risks inherent in trying something new. There are still times I feel insecure, terrified and inexperienced. I look forward to the day when I can say that my eduction is complete, but I am sure that it will never come, because where ever I get to, from that vantage point I can see further and the amount to learn about the whole fascinating field of women and men having babies is infinite.

So this book, teaching more practical skills for the midwife to help women through the pain of labour, suggesting more sensitive ways of addressing women and their partners going through stressful times, is of immense value, and I am pleased to have been asked to write the foreword to this fascinating book of Andrea's.

This book would have been enormously useful when I was training, and I have already found it useful now. We certainly had no lectures during my training on the "how to" of alternatives to drugs for pain relief in labour. I still carry Entonox in the boot of my car in case the woman wants a little something for her pain as she labours at home. The idea of using hot, wet towels to soothe and calm was totally new to me until I talked to Australian midwives and Andrea, and having now tried them, I can see what a wonderful invention they are.

As I have travelled the world representing the Royal College of Midwives, and acting as an ambassador for British midwifery overseas, I have been fortunate in having seen how midwives practise in other countries. They have a whole range of ideas and strategies that differ from mine, and some wonderful ideas, often borne of practical experience, that we could easily incorporate into our midwifery lexicon.

This book offers midwives a different perspective on birth (an Australian one, this time), with the chance to explore ideas, well proven elsewhere, that could benefit our pregnant women. Those of you who have participated in Andrea's wonderful workshops will already have had a taste of these, and this book will make them available to a wider audience.

Midwives everywhere need to learn from each other, to share and celebrate those special tricks of the trade that distinguish our practice from the current medical model so prevalent in our hospitals. I commend this book to you, and hope that it will stimulate your own curiosity about birth and your role in being "with woman". I am now off to heat up the next round of hot towels — the woman in the room next door sounds as if she is approaching transition!

Caroline Flint SRN SCM ADM

INTRODUCTION   1

Chapter 1
THE ROLE OF THE MIDWIFE   5

Chapter 2
FIRST DO NO HARM   11

Chapter 3
WHAT WAS THAT YOU SAID? THE LANGUAGE OF BIRTH   19

Chapter 4
TUNING IN TO WOMEN   25
    Women you don't like   31
    Women who are in a panic   31
    Supporting autonomy and discouraging dependence   33

Chapter 5
THE PHYSIOLOGY OF LABOUR AND BIRTH   39
    Oxytocin   40
    Endorphins   44
    Catecholamines   50
    The role of the pelvis in labour   53
    The fetus ejection reflex   53
    Adrenalin and the baby   54

Chapter 6
HOW CAN I HELP?   57
    The last week/s of pregnancy   58
    During first stage   60
    Transition   86
    Second Stage   92
    After the baby is born   104
    Managing complications   106

Chapter 7

SUPPORTING PARTNERS   117

Choosing support people   118
During the pregnancy   120
During labour   122
The needs of fathers   123
Other issues concerning support people   125
Siblings   127

Chapter 8

ACTING AS AN ADVOCATE   131

Informed choice   133
Opportunities for advocacy during pregnancy   135
During labour and birth   136
What about the legalities?   140
Reducing your legal vulnerability   144
Direct action as an advocate   145

Chapter 9

THE POTENTIAL OF
PRE-NATAL EDUCATION   149

Giving information   153
Pre-natal classes   155
Debriefing   159
Labour ward tours   161

Chapter 10

MAKING IT HAPPEN   165

Changing your personal practice   174

APPENDIX   177
INDEX   179

INTRODUCTION

As you pick up this book to explore its contents, you might have had two questions in your mind: why a book on the art of midwifery? and, why would a non-midwife take the liberty of writing about midwifery skills? Good questions — requiring answers, here at the beginning, so we can begin to develop a dialogue openly and thoughtfully.

For many years, I have been working as a childbirth educator, much of the time with parents in the usual ways, but increasingly with midwives. In the early 1980s when I began to explore the concepts of active, physiological birth and how this could be integrated into pre-natal classes that up until then had focused on training women to perform in labour, it gradually became apparent to me that women, left to their own devices and in the right kind of supportive environment, did not need to be taught, led or even "cared for" to any great extent during labour. At the births I attended as a support person, I noticed that women were quite capable of finding their own ways of giving birth, and that in the process they reinforced their own beliefs in themselves while discovering their strengths and gaining confidence. Sometimes, however, this did not happen, because the woman found herself caught up in a system of maternity care that imposed routine and impersonal processes. It was not that the caregivers, often the doctor, mostly the midwives, didn't *want* to offer the women a memorable and beautiful birth, it seemed they didn't know *how* this could be done, and that they had few ideas beyond the giving of drugs, for making labour easier for the women in their care.

I decided to turn my attention to these caregivers: if I could show them some alternative ways of being "with women", then labouring women and their babies would ultimately benefit. It was not that midwives enjoyed using

1

interventions (they often complained that birth was regimented), the problem was that they did not seem able to think of alternatives, or ways of creating the peace, privacy and protective surroundings that are the essential ingredients for an easy and safe birth. I developed a two-day workshop program, called "Active Birth" and offered midwives and other health professionals a chance to explore basic physiology and strategies for enhancing its actions during labour — in other words, ways of working with women's bodies, rather than against them. Many midwives commented that they had never learned these simple strategies in their midwifery training, and I replied that much of what we were exploring could only really be learned by observing and responding to individual women, rather than from dry, theoretical lectures. We explored the art of midwifery, not the theory or research, and the mechanisms of essential human physiology as they work in women giving birth.

Of course, we drew on the research as much as we could, and had at times to delve into the archives to find the studies that described birth biology. Much of the current research is devoted to examining the effects of the treatments that have been imposed on women and babies during birth, and few current researchers are interested in learning more about what is "normal". One conclusion that has been clearly demonstrated by modern research is that less intervention often gives better outcomes. These findings reinforce midwifery/social support, rather than the technological/medical methods in vogue in westernised maternity services.

This increasing acceptance of midwifery as a means of achieving better outcomes has created problems of its own. Midwives have been trained in hospitals, and therefore have little experience of normal birth physiology. They seem, at times, to practise more like obstetric nurses, and a tendency to resort to drugs for relieving pain in labour demonstrates how medicalised midwifery has become. It has been interesting to note how quickly the idea of using warm water baths in the labour wards for relieving pain in labour was adopted by midwives, especially in the United Kingdom. Here was a non-invasive alternative to drugs, which struck an immediate chord with midwives, and women. Its popularity is encouraging, showing how willingly midwives embrace low-tech, non-medical ways of supporting women during birth.

In addition to using warm water, there are other means midwives can use to enable women to birth easily and safely, and this book, based on the active birth workshops I have been presenting for many years, sets out to explore some of them. It is not, by any means, intended to be the final word, or even a comprehensive guide, since there will be as many ways of being with women as there are ways of giving birth. My aim is to fire your imagination and to encourage lateral thinking that will inspire you to experiment. Once you have established a trusting relationship with a woman, that is, you trust *her* ability to birth well, and she trusts *you* to stand by while she does it, the rapport that naturally evolves will facilitate your learning: she will show you how it can be done. This book describes some of the lessons I have learned from being with women having babies, and you will no doubt add your own insights as your experience grows.

In observing and learning from women during birth, one of my greatest assets has been the fact that I am not a midwife. My lack of a rigorous and strictly focused training has given me the freedom to just be there during birth with an open and accepting mind. I have been able to place all my attention on the women, their responses and needs, without having to be concerned with par-tograms, monitors, infusions, and the like. That does not mean I was doing nothing — maintaining concentration, sensitivity, energy and unobtrusive assistance can be quite arduous over many hours. A support person offers a continuous, uninterrupted presence and it is this commitment that brings its own reward for those who are curious about how birth happens, and observant of the intimacies of the process. It is also a great adventure, full of possibilities and unexpected discoveries.

I offer you these ideas as my way of supporting and promoting midwifery. I believe that the health and well being of our planet and our very lives depend on caring, empathetic people taking responsibility and working together for the betterment of us all. This process has its roots in birth, and midwives have a major role to play at this pivotal time. We humans need to achieve better birth outcomes as a demonstration of our commitment to the future. We must reduce intervention and pay more attention to protecting nature's intricate system for the survival of our species. A generous dose of love and compassion for our fellow beings, especially women striving to do their best in labour, would be one place to start.

Putting these ideas together would not have been possible without the help of a number of people. The women who invited me to be at their births have been my major source of inspiration. The midwives who have shared their insights and experience during workshops have also expanded my horizons. My staff, colleagues and my son have provided enormous support and encouragement at all times. I am deeply grateful to you all.

As you explore the ideas described here, perhaps they will trigger insights and memories of your own. Please share these with your own colleagues, and if you feel inclined, with me. I would welcome your feedback. Most of all, enjoy your work for what it offers: magic moments of rare beauty, excitement and never-ending wonderment. Aren't you glad you are a midwife?

Chapter 1

THE ROLE OF THE MIDWIFE

Midwifery is all about the art and skill of caring for childbearing women. As a calling it is one of the most essential in a community — for thousands of years women have relied on other women for assistance and comfort when giving birth and nurturing their babies. Some women in the communal group were recognised as having special attributes and qualities that made them particularly welcome around the time of birth and these women became midwives. They passed on their special expertise to others through on-the-job training, expanding their expertise by sharing "tricks of the trade" with each other and by learning from the women in their care.

The history and development of midwifery as a profession, its organisation, training and current position in society has been written about extensively by others (Gelis 1991; Rhodes 1995; Oakley 1986). The current struggles of midwifery to both retain and regain a foothold in the western medicalised health care system has also been documented, and although progress can be slow, advances are being made. The shifts in government policy in New Zealand, the United Kingdom and some States in the United States of America shows that midwives are again standing tall and taking their rightful place as primary caregivers for normal, healthy, pregnant women.

As midwives grow in political strength, they are finding themselves in new territory, charged with the responsibility of leading the team of carers at the service of pregnant and birthing women. Some have found this development exciting, fulfilling and rewarding, while others have found it daunting, challenging and frightening. The medicalisation of birth in western countries and its gradual centralisation in hospitals has eroded the training of midwives, who now learn about normal birth in very abnormal settings — the hospitals.

Thus instead of spending time sitting with women to observe and discover the many patterns of behaviour that are associated with uncomplicated birth, midwives are learning how to apply the technological gadgets used in hospitals to monitor progress. Their eyes are becoming accustomed to watching dials, graphs and printouts, instead of registering the subtle nuances of human behaviour displayed by women during pregnancy and birth in social, not medical surroundings.

The labours observed in these hospital settings have also been affected by the impact of the surroundings, so that the appearance of normal labour has been altered, usually in ways that are felt by labouring women to be more "acceptable" in the hospital environment. This fact has been recognised by the World Health Organisation, which stated in "Having a Baby in Europe (WHO 1985):

"...By 'medicalising' birth, i.e. separating a woman from her own environment and surrounding her with strange people using strange machines to do strange things to her in an effort to assist her (and much or all of this may sometimes be necessary), the woman's state of mind and body is so altered that her way of carrying through this intimate act must also be altered and the state of the baby born must equally be altered. The result is that it is no longer possible to know what births would have been like before these manipulations. Most health care providers no longer know what 'non-medicalised' birth is. This is an overwhelmingly important issue. Almost all women in most developed countries in Europe give birth in hospital, leaving the providers of birth services with no genuine yardstick against which to measure their care. What is the range of safe labour? What is the true (i.e. the absolute minimum) incidence of respiratory distress in newborn babies? What is the incidence of tears to the tissues surrounding the vaginal opening if the tissues are not first cut? What is the incidence of depression in women after 'non-medicalised' birth? The answer to all these, and many more questions is the same: no one knows. The entire modern obstetric and neonatal literature is essentially based on observations of 'medicalised' birth."

Learning about normal pregnancy and birth is almost impossible when it occurs in institutions, as not only do women behave differently, but their caregivers take on institutional roles, that befit their position and workplace setting. This subtle and pervasive conditioning of midwives has also been documented, for example by Sheila Hunt in her excellent exposé of labour ward norms "The Social Meaning of Midwifery" (Hunt 1995).

One of the most insidious effects of the medicalisation of birth, then, is that midwives are not learning about normal pregnancy and birth behaviours, since these are almost impossible to observe when women give birth in hospitals. The inhibition of labouring women's behaviour, the rigid application of protocols and policies and the professional limitations placed on midwives all conspire to systematically undermine midwifery in the most basic skills needed: the art of being "with women". Midwives may have excellent credentials in monitor watching, medication management, drip insertion, assessment, suturing, charting and physical examination, but they may lack the ability to observe, interpret, support, encourage, wait and understand that can only come from training gained in a non-medicalised setting. Some midwives will have the opportunity to learn their craft apprentice-style in the community and their skills will be many and varied as a result. It is a sad reflection that on the whole, midwives who have learned in this way are treated with suspicion, since their insights and expertise are often different from those gained by midwives trained in hospital systems. A midwife who has learned her craft in the community alone may not be as well versed in monitor reading and medication management. However, since these are largely skills associated with medical management of birth, it could be argued that she does not need these skills: if the birth has strayed from normal to the extent that a developing problem needs close assessment and evaluation, this specialised care would be better given by those with medical training anyway.

Midwifery education was traditionally based in practical problem solving. Midwives, in common with women in general, were illiterate, and therefore they did not record their observations in written form. They learned from each other informally, passing on useful tips, and learning by practise and evaluation — the basis of experiential learning. Midwifery education, once it was established in formal school settings, became focused on technical topics, taking a leaf from the medical training given to doctors. The early midwifery schools were supervised by doctors, who made up their advisory bodies and oversaw curriculum development. Incorporating midwifery skills used in the community by generations of women would have been out of place in this "modern" approach, and the skills themselves unknown by those in teaching roles.

The current trend towards evidence based practice is long overdue for medicine, especially in the field of pregnancy and childbirth. Science can and should measure the impact of intervention so women can assess the benefits and risks of proposed treatments. We must be careful, however, to recognise that many basic midwifery skills are beyond the limits of scientific enquiry. "Caring" is a concept that cannot be researched as it is entirely linked to an individual woman and her specific needs. In addition, there is no need to research the value of basic physiology — thousands of years of evolution have already refined the process extensively. One has only to look at the way in which humans have increased and multiplied, even in the poorest of conditions, to see that it is a very successful process. What is needed, however, is

Maternity care behaviours: the medical model vs the social model	
In the medical model, carers:	In the social model, carers:
• Give advice	• Offer suggestions, listen
• Regard themselves as experts	• Regard themselves as peers
• Are centred on themselves, their knowledge	• Are on equal terms, not dominant
• Expect compliance	• Invite participation
• Make few allowances for individual needs	• Are centred on client's needs, not their own ideas
• Take charge	• Provide support, are available on request
• Set up the pattern for care	• Encourage client responsibility
• Focus narrowly towards a diagnosis	• Encourage lateral thinking, holistic views
• Are punitive towards mistakes make by client	• Are accepting of mistakes, use them as a basis for learning
• Disempower	• Empower

more investigation into the intricate physiology of human reproductive behaviour, since further insights might give us clues about why non-interventionist midwifery approaches work well, and also explain the reason why so many labours develop complications as a result of "expert" medical care.

Sending midwives out to work in the community to expand their skills and develop their confidence and trust in normal physiologic birth may also present problems. With the socialisation of midwives into the medical model of birth found in hospitals, many will feel ill-equipped to assist at births without their usual props, and their resultant anxiety may undermine the opportunity for learning, and at the same time disturb the woman's birth physiology. An apprenticeship system, using experienced community based midwives would offer one solution, but this doubling of resources may be an expensive option for underfunded health systems.

In reality, today's midwives need to have skills appropriate to birth in hospital settings, plus insights that can only be gained from learning acquired in the community. Midwives will need to be adaptable, since most women will give birth in hospital for the time being. For women to successfully labour in this setting a caregiver with a midwifery (social model) approach rather than one whose practice is based on the medical model will be crucial. Pregnant and labouring women also have a right to the kind of care they would have received if they had stayed in their own homes to give birth — they should not have to endure a medicalised birth just because they are in hospital. Thus the midwife needs to use her skills to establish a birth place setting that enhances rather than undermines normal physiology. She needs to draw on her experience of women labouring at home to enable her to assess when labour is progressing in a "normal" fashion, and as a means of alerting her to labour behaviours that indicate abnormal responses and potential problems. "Keeping labour normal" is a primary goal of the midwife — not an easy task in the hospital, with all its influences on maternal and staff behaviours. Learning what can be considered "normal" is another challenge, one that can provide a lifetime of professional excitement and stimulation for the interested midwife.

The role of the midwife is to accompany a woman on the journey through pregnancy and birth and be available as she adjusts to her new baby. The role has many facets, requiring resourcefulness that will vary according to the woman and her needs. How can midwives embrace their full potential and hone their expertise in assisting with normal pregnancy and birth? Defining one's professional aims and objectives will help illuminate the way ahead: clearly enunciating one's philosophy and guiding principles; describing the overall framework of one's personal practice; listing the skills already acquired and identifying those areas where further training is needed; describing desired outcomes for oneself and the women; formulating a job description; and identifying the scope and limits of professional responsibility. These are all steps relevant to any professional person's growth and development.

As these personal needs and plans are developed, it is important to remember some basic truths, related specifically to midwifery:

- All reproductive behaviours are designed to be as successful and rewarding as possible, to ensure the species increases and multiplies.
- Evolutionary pressures have ensured that the system works.
- All women are born with innate knowledge about how to grow and give birth to a baby, breastfeed and nurture their children.
- Birth is a normal process, infinitely variable and highly individual for women.
- Midwifery offers a holistic approach to the care of women during childbearing, with the emphasis on maintaining the normalcy of the physiologic process.

The craft of the midwife has to be learned in settings where women are able to behave in physiologically appropriate ways. Only then will midwives be able to recognise when birth is deviating from the normal process and requires medical assistance.

The following chapters are intended to resurrect some of the basic "know-how" needed by all those who assist at birth. The suggestions are by no means comprehensive, since midwives all over the world have accumulated handy hints and useful techniques to enable birth to proceed normally. The ideas outlined here are based on personal experience in a western, medicalised system of largely hospital based birth, and have proven useful in enabling the women concerned to give birth with few, if any, interventions. Creativity and lateral thinking are the hallmarks of problem based learning, and an inquiring mind and observant eye can trigger much useful learning. There is much to discover!

References

Gelis J. 1991, *History of Childbirth*, Polity Press and Basil Blackwell, UK.

Hunt S. & Symonds A. 1995, *The Social Meaning of Midwifery*, Mosby, UK.

Oakley A. 1986, *The Captured Womb*, Basil Blackwell, UK.

Rhodes P. 1995, *A Short History of Clinical Midwifery*, Books for Midwives Press, UK.

World Health Organisation 1985, *Having a Baby in Europe*, Public Health in Europe 26, Denmark.

Chapter 2

FIRST DO NO HARM

Surely this dictum, written for the medical profession, could not be relevant for midwives! In the sense that midwives should not be prescribing and carrying out medical treatments, it may be of less direct concern. However, midwives do find themselves using medically indicated procedures and are often responsible for giving medication. In addition, many of the apparently innocuous interventions overseen or used by midwives have effects that could justify this timely warning. The list of possible non-medical interventions includes many basic or routine procedures that have the potential of disturbing or even frightening women in labour. Their commonplace nature and familiarity poses additional risks, as these factors increase the chance that caregivers will overlook their possible impact, especially when occurring to a woman already uneasy in unfamiliar surroundings. All of them, in addition to the well-known medical interventions, could possibly cause unintentional harm.

Attention to this issue of unintentional harm has been drawn by Michel Odent (Odent 1994), who has described the "nocebo effect". He writes:

"While everybody knows about the 'Placebo effect', its opposite, the 'Nocebo effect' is rarely mentioned. Nocebo, from the Latin, originally means: 'I shall do harm'. There is a nocebo effect when the doctor or anybody else does more harm than good by interfering with someone's fantasy life, imagination or beliefs.

"It is now recognised that a certain style of prenatal care, constantly focusing on potential problems, can have a negative effect on the well being of pregnant women, and therefore on the health of their babies."

Potential interventions in childbirth

- Giving birth in hospital
- Labouring on the bed
- Giving birth on the bed
- Wearing other people's clothes (hospital gowns etc.)
- Internal examinations
- Baseline electronic fetal monitoring
- Restrictions on companions
- Restrictions on food and drink
- Imposition of time limits
- Learned relaxation techniques
- Imposed breathing patterns
- Distraction techniques
- Eye contact with the labouring woman
- Being moved from place to place during labour
- Constant checking of the baby's heartbeat
- Being left alone in a strange place
- Change of staff during labour
- Lack of privacy

The implications of his observations for midwifery are interesting. The constant referral of women for prenatal tests to look for possible problems, the fear that certain words (such as "gestational diabetes", or "breech") engender in both the women and their caregivers, the application of routine procedures which may be misinterpreted by women are all examples cited by Michel Odent in outlining his theory that better outcomes can be achieved by emphasising the positive, rather than highlighting the negative. The effects on women of the language used in childbirth will be explored in Chapter 3.

One result of the blending of midwifery care into the medical model has been the development of double standards — messages that state one thing but mean another in reality. The lack of clear cut aims and objectives for maternity care and the territorial battleground between midwives and doctors for the right to manage births has caused conflicting advice to be given to women and muddled thinking amongst caregivers. The list below highlights a selection of current double standards in maternity care, and is not intended to be exhaustive. Evaluation of many facets of treatment regimes compared with instructions or advice given to pregnant women will no doubt reveal others.

Some examples of double standards in maternity care

Statement	*Reality*
"Don't take drugs during your pregnancy — they may harm your unborn baby"	"In labour you can have any drugs you need — they have little, if any effect on the baby"
"It is your baby, your birth — you must take responsibility and make your own decisions"	"Our protocols dictate that you: must be induced after 24 hours without contractions following your membranes rupturing; have oxytocics for third stage; have routine electronic fetal monitoring on admission; give your baby Vitamin K; have your membranes ruptured at 4 cm of dilatation ..."
"You have a right to make your own decisions about your care"	"We will be happiest if you make decisions with which we agree"
"We are always right and never make mistakes"	"We do make mistakes, but we don't want you to know about them"
"Don't lie down on your back during pregnancy — it compromises the placental circulation and may affect the baby"	"Just lie down: while we attach the monitor; check your dilatation; rupture your membranes; deliver your baby."
"If you rupture your membranes at 30 weeks of pregnancy, we will give you antibiotics and try to forestall the labour"	"If you rupture your membranes at 40 weeks of pregnancy, we want to get your baby born as soon as possible"

In canvassing the obvious medical avenues as causes of unintentional harm, the giving of medications is a conspicuous example. There are a number of drugs that are given to pregnant and labouring women by midwives: valium to calm and induce sleep; pethidine to sedate and relax during labour; nitrous oxide and oxygen during transition for pain; oxytocics for the speedy conclusion of third stage and to forestall possible bleeding. Other drugs may be prescribed by an attending doctor, and these will most likely be administered by the midwife on the doctor's behalf. The extent of this problem is reflected in the outcomes reported for midwifery care, particularly in the United Kingdom. Whilst current political change has ensured that in the UK 75% of women giving birth will be attended primarily by a midwife, up to 98% of women are receiving drugs for pain relief in labour (Page 1996; Hundley et al. 1994). Of this group, between 16% and 32% will have an epidural (RCOG annual report, 1993), leaving the majority of women being given either pethidine or nitrous oxide. In other countries, where midwives practice more autonomously, such as The Netherlands, New Zealand and in the birth centres of Australia and the United States outcomes reflect the use of alternative means of pain relief rather than a reliance on drugs (Harvey et al. 1996; Rowley et al. 1995; Lydon-Rochelle 1995).

The Federal Food and Drug Administration in the United States bluntly stated over 20 years ago that "No drug has been proven safe for the unborn baby". Nothing has happened in the succeeding years to make them alter this pronouncement, and the paucity of research on the effects of drugs on newborns shows that very few people seem to be sufficiently concerned about the effects on babies to carry out scientific evaluation. In addition women are being denied information they need to form the basis of an informed decision about using drugs during labour.

This situation is a good example of the practical implications of the double standards that exist in maternity care. Women are exhorted, bullied, encouraged, even prosecuted in some cases in the United States, for taking drugs during the pregnancy that could be harmful for their unborn babies, yet when these same women arrive in the hospital to give birth, they are offered a number of drugs with little or no mention of the potential effects on the baby! It is as if the baby has suddenly ceased to be sensitive to drugs, or that drugs sanctioned by the staff in the hospital are acceptable and innocuous, while anything taken by the mother on her own initiative is dangerous and harmful. Those who have taken very good care of themselves and their babies through thoughtful modification of their diets and lifestyles for nine months could easily find this double standard confusing and undermining. Perhaps in the future the legal ramifications of this conflicting advice will also be clarified.

Many midwives find themselves in the invidious position of being told they must follow hospital policies on these issues, or risk censure. Policies and protocols have been established by hospital administrations in an attempt to reduce legal risk and encourage a uniform approach to management. Rigorous adherence to protocols and the application of generalised policies will not protect against possible litigation — quite the contrary. Since labour and birth are highly individual in nature, complications are likely to be affected by individual circumstances as well. It is not possible to make labours uniform in the same way as the treatment of medical conditions — birth is a normal bodily function, not an illness. The most famous example of trying to make labours uniform is the Active Management of Labour protocol (O'Driscoll & Meagher 1980), instituted in Dublin to better manage a large number of births with very few facilities. While it may be possible to have all labours completed within given time frames, whilst retaining desirable medical results (low caesarean section rates), the cost to the women, in emotional and psychological terms was not canvassed, these outcomes being assumed to be positive by the doctors themselves.

Legal protection is not afforded by blanket policies. The issue of informed consent has been tested in a number of landmark legal cases (Rogers vs Whittaker, 1991 was the first in Australia), and establishes that no treatment of any kind can be undertaken without the patient giving consent based on *their* assessment of the risks involved. Thus policies such as the routine injection of oxytocics for third stage cannot be carried out on the basis that it is hospital policy. Every woman must give her specific consent based on information about the benefits and risks. To do otherwise would leave the hospital and caregivers open to a potential charge of negligence or assault. A similar situation exists with procedures such as rupturing of membranes, and administration of Vitamin K to the newborn, amongst others. Every midwife needs to appraise herself of the legalities surrounding informed consent, and a number of publications are available (Frith 1996; Beech 1991; Libesman & Sripathy 1996; Dimond 1994; Jones 1994). This issue is explored further in Chapter 8.

For the midwife, another dilemma arises when she is asked to carry out a treatment prescribed by a doctor. Although the doctor may carry the ultimate responsibility if results of the treatment are questioned, the midwife may be challenged on the basis that as a professional person she should have had some knowledge of the potential problems that could have been incurred. This potential scenario is particularly pertinent to doctors' private patients, especially where the doctor leaves "standing orders" for the midwife to carry out in his absence. At least with private patients, the lines of responsibility are clear, and there is no reason why a midwife should carry out any treatment on the doctor's behalf: the contract exists between the doctor and his patient, with the doctor liable for his actions. In any situation where the midwife is being asked to perform a medical treatment she is quite justified, even obliged, to ask the doctor to discuss the procedure in full with the patient in order to obtain fully informed consent. The doctor could also be called on to carry out the procedure. There are many situations when this issue can arise, such as induction of labour for non-medical reasons, routine rupturing of membranes, the giving of pain medications and routine internal examinations. Instead of blindly following the stated protocol, the midwife can ask the doctor to see the patient, to firstly explain the proposed procedure, then carry it out. In this way, the midwife can be seen to be protecting the woman from a treatment for which no proper consent has been given, she is ensuring that women are given the information they need to make an informed choice, she is protecting her profession by demonstrating her commitment to protecting and supporting normal physiology (not the medical model), and she is affording the doctor a chance to reduce his exposure to a potential legal challenge. Private patients are usually better placed to issue a legal challenge as they have the education, the money and the expertise. Doctors need to recognise that their systematic over servicing of this segment of the community (as reflected in birth outcome statistics) is potentially very risky, especially in a climate of increasing scrutiny from knowing consumers with a litigious outlook on life.

Where the midwife has sole charge of a maternity case, the situation is different. Here, the midwife is responsible for her own actions and for the safety of mother and baby. Adequate training, supportive resources and appropriate backup are necessary for the protection of the midwife. Systems are in place for this in the United Kingdom, New Zealand, The Netherlands and other European countries. Elsewhere, where legislation does not exist, or regulations have not been formulated for births in all potential settings (especially out-of-hospital births), midwives' professional bodies provide some support and assistance.

Sometimes, even midwifery care can have untoward effects for the mother and baby. Some of these outcomes will stem from an incomplete understanding of the physiology of labour and birth, while others will result from non-intentional intervention in the normal process. Midwives need a good working knowledge of the various hormones that guide and protect the woman's behaviour during pregnancy and birth. Although it is difficult to find this information in standard midwifery and obstetric textbooks, Chapter 5 offers a summary of the main points. With the knowledge about the importance of oxytocin, endorphins, adrenalin and nor-adrenalin during pregnancy and birth as a foundation, it becomes possible to assess the impact of disturbances on the birth process. Strategies for either avoiding or repairing the damage can then be devised. Later chapters offer some suggestions in this regard.

Many of the ministrations offered by midwives have the intention of supporting or caring for women during pregnancy and labour. How these actions might be interpreted by the women concerned are less clear. For one woman, the attention might be welcome and beneficial, while for another, the outcome might be unwanted distraction and the upsetting of her physiology. Neither she, nor the attending midwife can tell in advance what the outcome will be — perhaps exercising caution should be the overriding approach. Making assumptions is always risky, the one constant being that in almost all cases, the natural process of pregnancy and birth has an enormous drive for success and if left undisturbed, encompasses in-built fail-safe mechanisms to achieve a positive outcome.

Caution needs to be extended to the use of birth plans. Although very useful, as we shall see in later chapters, they must be viewed as guidelines to the woman's preferences, and written with a broad perspective that enables free- dom of choice at all stages and times. Prescriptive birth plans are similar to hospital protocols — they both presume an outcome and take no account of individuality or changing circumstances.

How then, should a midwife proceed, if she wishes to "do no harm"? Perhaps the first step is to develop her trust and faith in the normal process of child- bearing. This will come from experience of pregnancy and birth gained from observing many different labours, preferably in settings that enable normal physiology to flower. Sharing stories and passing "helpful hints" amongst colleagues is a way of increasing personal experience more quickly. Learning from other midwives in this way is a valid step in the gaining of insight.

Avoiding medical interventions is also a logical step. The giving of drugs and the carrying out of invasive procedures are not practises of midwifery — they belong to the medical model of care. Learning about alternative ways to increase womens' comfort and confidence, and non-pharmacological ways of reducing pain are essential, though these alternatives must always be seen as possible interventions in themselves, depending on their effect on individual women. Alternative therapies, homoeopathic remedies, acupuncture, aroma- therapy and even prescribed breathing patterns are all potentially invasive, and many have not been proven scientifically valid or even safe.

Not sanctioning inappropriate treatments, and refusing to carry out treat- ments on the behalf of other practitioners will also protect women from unnecessary interference. Developing strategies for managing these situa- tions will be a challenge for the profession as a whole as well as for individual midwives. Perhaps the curricula in training courses could be expanded to include a solid foundation in the development of student competencies in negotiation and conflict resolution, counselling and communication.

Checking the research and staying abreast of the scientific evidence will strengthen the midwife's practice. Demanding that hospital policies and pro- tocols are based on available (and changing) evidence is a necessary, if diffi- cult and confrontational task. To support an unjust and unscientific protocol, without challenging its basis, is not only unkind to women, it is inappropriate for midwifery and its professionalism. Methods of challenging the system in this way need to be explored so that plans of action can be developed and enacted.

Doing no harm is a worthy, yet difficult aim to achieve. It will test the resolve of midwives both collectively and individually, yet its accomplishment will reap enormous benefits for women and their babies. At its most basic level, midwifery is not about giving drugs and performing medical procedures. The skill of the midwife is in offering personalised care based on the woman's needs, that does not disturb the physiologic processes of birth or carry potential for harm to the mother and baby. It is this type of care that the vast majority of women in the world have recognised as essential, and which increasing numbers of western women are demanding.

References

Beech B. 1991, *Who's Having Your Baby?*, Bedford Square Press, UK.

Dimond B. 1994, *The Legal Aspects of Midwifery*, Books for Midwives Press, UK.

Frith L. 1996, *Ethics and Midwifery*, Butterworth, UK.

Harvey S., Jarrell J., Brant R., Stainton C. & Rach D. 1996, 'A Randomized, Controlled Trial of Nurse-Midwifery Care', *Birth*, vol. 23, no. 3.

Hundley V., Cruickshank F., et al. 1994, 'Midwife managed delivery unit: a randomised controlled comparison with consultant led care', *BMJ*, vol. 309, pp. 1400–4.

Jones S. 1994, *Ethics in Midwifery*, Mosby, UK.

Libesman T. & Sripathy V. 1996, *Your Body Your Baby*, Redfern Legal Publishing Centre, Sydney.

Lydon-Rochelle M. 1995, 'Cesarean delivery rates in women cared for by certified nurse-midwives in the United States: A review', *Birth*, vol. 22, pp. 211–219.

Odent M. 1994, 'Launching CENEP', *Primal Health Research Newsletter*, vol. 2, no. 2.

O'Driscoll K. & Meagher D. 1980, *Active Management of Labour*, W. B. Saunders, London.

Rowley M., Hensley M., Brinsmead M. & Wlodarcyzk J. 1996, 'Continuity of care by a midwife team versus routine care during pregnancy and birth: A randomised trial', *Med J Aust*, vol. 163, pp. 289–293.

Royal College of Obstetricians and Gynaecologists 1995, *Annual statistical return report taken from the 1993 statistics*, RCOG London.

Chapter 3

WHAT WAS THAT YOU SAID? THE LANGUAGE OF BIRTH

We communicate with each other in many ways: verbally, non-verbally, emotionally and instinctively.

Much has been written about the language of birth, the words that are used to describe the various facets of childbearing and the techniques used to manage it (Leap 1992; Oakley 1980; Davis-Floyd 1992; Pfeuffer Kahn 1995). Since the first books on midwifery were written by men and most of the vocabulary was drawn from medicine, the picture created is one of a process beset with problems and mystery, resulting from its interpretation by alien eyes. There also seems to be more than a touch of womb envy about the systematic debunking of the creative energy displayed by women as they give birth!

There are many reasons why this happened. Women generally were considered unworthy of an education and were therefore largely illiterate until relatively recent times, so they had no means of recording their experiences with childbirth. Medical men, anxious to take over this female domain and gain further status through their involvement in the creative process, put their particular stamp on the language. Women kept childbirth matters largely to themselves, seeing it as primarily women's work that they did not think was appropriate to share with men. This secrecy, although important to female culture and bonding amongst the women, may have contributed to its allure as an object for male domination by creating a powerful mystique around the process.

As a result of these developments, today's women's business is discussed using terminology that is largely masculine, medical and negative. Women can be left with the impression that childbearing is difficult, demeaning, unpleasant and even hostile, just because of the words we use to describe how our bodies give birth. Although the language has been created by men, midwives have fallen into the trap of perpetuating this situation through their wholesale adoption of the vocabulary. Words have a powerful ability to alter perception and create impressions. If we reassess the words we use and substitute more women-friendly terms, we could, in addition to achieving more positive impressions generally about birth, alter our beliefs and attitudes towards birth.

Communication, however, is more than just the words that we speak. The way we verbalise, the tone of our voice and the emphasis or stress we use, colours the way our words are received and interpreted by the listener. The most important outcome of communication is the message received by the listener — if the recipient gets the wrong message then our communication has failed. Here, the problem lies not with the receiver, but with the sender, who must now try either different words, or a different approach altogether, to get the message across. Let's explore some examples:

Tone: Try saying: "She's the woman who wants an active birth" with excitement in your voice. Now try it with a sneer, as though you disapprove.

Emphasis: Imagine saying this sentence several times with the emphasis on a different word each time: "**She** wants a vaginal birth after a previous caesarean". "She **wants** a vaginal birth after a previous caesarean". "She wants a **vaginal** birth after a previous caesarean". "She wants a vaginal birth after a **previous caesarean**". If you added a different tone in your voice as well, imagine the impact you would have!

Evaluating specific words is also an interesting and vital exercise. One of the most commonly used words in the childbirth vocabulary is the word "delivery". Its universal use signifies its total acceptance by the professional community. What constitutes a "delivery"? It is a task or service performed by others, an impersonal task more befitting a letter than a baby. The acceptance and use of this one word also identifies the power play in operation during birth — "just lie there while we take your baby then give it to you (when we are ready)". This may not be the intention of the midwife, but by using the word "delivery" any ideas of the woman giving birth herself are neatly sidestepped or undermined. There is not one occasion when the word "birth" cannot be used instead. Just eliminating this one word from your daily conversations with women will help them feel more positive about what they will be doing and remind you of your position as an assistant in the process. Midwives can safely discard "I had a lovely delivery last night" and say instead "I was at a lovely birth last night". "She had a wonderful delivery" can safely become "She gave birth wonderfully". We no longer need "Delivery Suites" in our hospitals — they are "Maternity Units", "Birth Centres" or "Birth Suites" (perhaps a natural extension of the "Honeymoon Suite"). Once we have substituted "birth" for every example of "delivery" in our conversation, written works and medical records, we will have made some very basic progress towards normalising birth.

There are many other examples that are worthy of close attention. Apart from obviously degrading descriptions such as "the elderly primigravida" and "the incompetent cervix", inaccurate terms such as "failure to progress" and the outright labelling of "the VBAC" or "the Breech", derogatory terms such as "girls" or "mums" or "bubs" demonstrate condescension. It is "women" who have babies, and their status should be recognised in our choice of words.

Sometimes it is not just the terminology we use, but other small words that can creep in to our conversation that creates the negative image. The word "only", for example can be devastating: "She is only 3 centimetres dilated" can spell defeat to a woman in labour. "Still" also causes problems: "Are you still here?" said to a woman during a long labour can destroy confidence. How would you feel if, at 8 months of pregnancy, someone said to you "Just pop into the loo and do a wee". This sounds like "baby talk", the kind of patronising instruction that is given to a small child who has limited understanding.

Evaluating your own performance as a communicator takes courage. It is a process with its own rewards (such as fewer misunderstandings and a feeling of greater empathy with others) and is worthwhile in terms of personal professional development. There are a number of ways it can be undertaken.

Each time you are conversing with a woman in a professional capacity, notice what she is telling you by her facial expression. See what she is doing with her eyes — are they open and alert (a signal she is following you) or narrowed and clouded (which may mean she doesn't understand)? Note when any changes to her expression occur. What were you saying at the time? What were your actual words? Was it that you used a term she didn't understand, or did you add a phrase or word that had an emotional impact on her? Did you make a value-laden statement, or sound judgemental?

Sometimes we say one thing and mean another — be careful of your non-verbal messages as well as the words you are using. The non-verbal message often creates a stronger impression, and this will be registered by the listener, usually unconsciously, to see if it matches the spoken words. When a mismatch occurs, the listener will be confused and the message will not necessarily be interpreted as intended.

When you are examining the woman, for example, be aware that while you are performing your check, she will be intently studying your face. Any flicker of the eyebrow, narrowing of the eyes or hint of a frown and she may think there is a problem. Even the speed at which you enter a room, the smart efficiency with which you take her blood pressure, the flourish with which you straighten the bedclothes could create an impression of haste, of cold professionalism and distance, when warmth and empathy is what she seeks.

The level of your voice is also important. As we shall explore in the next chapter, being able to establish rapport with labouring women is an important skill for midwives to cultivate. Lowering your voice, even whispering, preserves a calm and peaceful atmosphere. Loud voices, even chirpy, cheerful tones can intrude on her quiet reverie and destroy concentration.

In general, the fewer words said during labour the better. Choose your words carefully, with a view to keeping the communication simple, honest and positive. Take note of the impact of your message: Was it understood? Have you created confusion? Have you made her anxious? If you need to clarify your message because it was not understood, try using a different way of getting through. For example, instead of giving her a potentially confusing description of how her baby is lying (posterior, or breech), use a fetal doll and placenta to show her. A simple diagram, especially when the woman speaks another language, could save time and confusion.

When explaining medical interventions or procedures, remember that it is the woman who must make the informed decision about her care. In giving her the information she may need, you need to be aware that the way in which you present the information can have a huge impact, perhaps even undermining her right to a free choice. Pay particular attention to:

➡ Making sure your information is based on the scientific evidence, and not hearsay or personal experience.

➡ Including all the pros and cons of the treatment or procedure. Avoid censoring or filtering the information.

➡ Letting the facts speak for themselves. Giving percentages, for example, instead of scary stories may enable a woman to better assess risk factors.

➡ Being aware of your own personal views towards the treatment being offered. Your own bias will show up in the words you choose and the way you speak them.

➡ Keeping the communication simple. Further details can always be added in response to questions or to clarify if requested by the woman.

➡ Noting when you have not been able to get your message across (you can tell from the look on her face and other non-verbal cues), choose a different medium — try a drawing, use a model, demonstrate on your own body etc.

➡ Allowing time for consideration and further questions before asking for her decision. Private time without the presence of caregivers is essential (except in real emergencies) and will ensure that better decisions are made, without duress.

You can check how you are being received either directly with the women you are talking to ("Did I make myself clear?", "I get the feeling I have confused you", "I didn't explain that well, did I?" etc.) or you could call on a colleague to assess your performance ("How did you think that explanation went?", "I am not sure I really got through to her — what did you think?"). It takes trust and openness to work with a colleague in this way, but you can be mutually useful to each other, and you will both be gaining professional skills in the process.

Feedback from women after the birth, either as part of a debriefing session or even in a formal evaluation (questionnaire) can give you useful insight into your performance. If this feedback is sought verbally, you will need to use your listening skills to elicit accurate responses especially of her feelings about her care. Questionnaires will need to be constructed with open ended questions and include requests for negative comments. Anonymity will make it easier for people to give negative feedback. People sometimes dislike being totally frank about negative aspects of their care (women seem to be particularly reticent in offering criticism, especially just after the birth) so phrasing questions in the positive, even when you are seeking negative reactions might help. Try asking "What would you change about your care next time?" or "How would you like the midwife to support you in your next birth?" or "How did you feel about the assistance offered to you by the staff in the Unit?".

Another way of improving communication and developing insight into women's needs is by using birth plans. Giving women the opportunity to state their wishes in this formal way serves to establish a flexible contract that takes some of the guesswork out of maternity care. Written guidelines can also enable you to act as an advocate and protector of women more easily, and this will be explored further in Chapter 8.

Sometimes, I have thought that non-English speakers may have a particular advantage in our labour wards. Unable to understand what they are being told, women just get on with having babies, and do well as long as no problem occurs. This may be one reason why the birth outcomes registered in hospitals serving migrant groups in the Sydney region (a very multicultural community) (NSW Department of Health 1993) are so much better than birth outcomes in hospitals situated in nearby suburbs with affluent, well educated populations. Yes, women do have a right to know, and yes, we usually do try to give women the information in ways they can understand. But at a basic level, when giving birth, women don't need a lot of talk, they need caring support so they can do the job themselves. The famous British slogan of the Second World War seems appropriate: "Careless talk costs lives!"

References

Davis-Floyd R. 1992, *Birth as an American Right of Passage*, University of California Press, USA.

Leap N. 1992, 'The power of words', *Nursing Times*, vol. 88, no. 21, pp. 60–61.

NSW Department of Health 1993, *The Health of Mothers born in Non-English Speaking Countries and their Babies NSW 1990–1993*, NSW Government, Sydney.

Oakley A. 1980, *Women Confined*, Martin Robinson, UK.

Pfeufer Kahn R. 1995, *Bearing Meaning — the language of birth*, University of Illinois Press, USA.

Chapter 4

TUNING IN TO WOMEN

Midwives are often assumed to have a natural gift for getting in tune with women and many do have a special affinity with women during pregnancy and birth. Perhaps it is the simple fact that midwives are usually women that facilitates this process — all women are born with basic reproductive abilities, including the necessary information on how to give birth and breastfeed, and this common knowledge forms a common thread connecting all women everywhere. Having insight and empathy for childbearing women is made easier when a caregiver possesses similar instincts which can be used to forge an understanding between them. This innate heritage enables women to form easy alliances and develop a deep understanding. It may also explain why men, who have different reproductive instincts, often find it difficult to feel at ease or to empathise with pregnant women.

Whilst being able to get in touch with women's needs may be easier for midwives (who are usually female), it is not always a straightforward process. Many factors can influence effective connection: differing cultural backgrounds; varying levels of personal experience; personality clashes; unhelpful training; pressures on the professional relationship; even lack of time or interest. Sometimes, assumptions being made on both sides will stand in the way of an easy and accepting working relationship. Hospital routines and protocols also block effective interactions, based as they are, on a broad perspective of birth rather than individual need.

Midwives need to develop an awareness of how their professional training and the structures of their workplace affect their work. These influences can be pervasive and detrimental, not only for the women giving birth in the institution, but to the staff, who can develop a blinkered view of birth that is dehumanising and disempowering. This is well illustrated by the aftermath of a "different" birth in a hospital (for example, the first birth where the woman uses a mat on the floor rather than the bed, or the first accidental waterbirth in the bath). Instead of celebrating a different and unique outcome, suspicion and scorn may pour down on the attending midwife, when the woman steps outside the hospital protocols and policies. This is reinforced by the labelling of many women in advance "she's the NCT woman", "she's the one who wants to bring her other children", or on a historical note "she's the one who wants the father at the birth!". The way these attitudes, beliefs and work practices develop and the effect they have is admirably described by Sheila Hunt (Hunt 1995), who reveals the inner workings of two large maternity units in the United Kingdom. The sad picture of impersonal care revealed by Hunt is played out in most institutional settings, and it stifles both professional growth and maternal instinct.

Much has been written about the need for *support* of women in pregnancy and birth. This term can be interpreted in many ways. In a physiological sense, there is little anyone can do to support the process since the uterus contracts as an involuntary muscle, over which there can be no direct control. Usually, the word support implies that the woman needs assistance, help, personal attention or physical comfort from others around her. Again, at a physiological level, her body will do its work in the most efficient way possible for her and her baby's needs. If, by "support", we mean emotional and psychological assistance — the giving of encouragement, the offering of soothing words to provide verbal analgesia, the creating of a permissive atmosphere in which she can behave instinctively — these actions are really manifestations of love. Women's bodies work best in labour when they are left undisturbed, free of distraction and in an atmosphere of total privacy. The kind words and soothing massage may unintentionally get in the way of these primal needs for peace and protection during birth, and slow rather than speed the birth. Providing the right amount of "support" can be a difficult juggling act, requiring sensitivity, tact and insight.

Perhaps we need to redefine the word "support" in the context of birth. Support can be provided in many ways, and when the normalcy of birth is accepted and the physiology of labour is understood, then perhaps the only "support" a woman needs is permission to follow her instincts. The primary role becomes one of establishing a protective shield around her so that she is not disturbed or distracted by any outside influence. With this kind of buffer in place, a feeling of safety is generated, and this in turn will enable the labour hormones, especially oxytocin and endorphin to flow, unhindered by adrenalin. Establishing this buffer, particularly in unfamiliar and alien environments such as hospital labour wards, takes effort and attention to detail. The ways this can be achieved are outlined in Chapter 6.

In the United States, a new health professional, the doula, has emerged to offer support and comfort to women during labour. Traditionally, this kind of presence was provided by the woman's family and friends, with the midwife acting as professional back up. The arrival on the scene of trained "support people" is more evidence of the medicalisation of birth. It seems that providing companionship, love, and practical assistance can no longer be left to the untrained — even this form of one-to-one help that happens naturally within the family, has been taken over by the professionals. The reliance on experts, even for the most basic of human comforts is perhaps symptomatic of a more general lack of confidence in normal social interactions. The selling of the need for a professional doula once again undermines a woman's belief that she can give birth by herself, and is a subtle form of disempowerment for women. Health professionals may want to act as rescuers of women in labour, but they should learn restraint, as every intervention on their part, from the simple (such as suggesting a professional support person is necessary to hold her hand and "guide" her through her labour), to the complex, (such as many obstetric interventions) devalues the power, strength and ability of women to give birth successfully. The systematic removal of women's powers has been a common goal of many societies.

Apart from immediate close family and friends, it has usually been to the midwife that the woman in labour turns for protection. The midwife understands the huge range of possibilities present in normal labour and the wide variety of responses demonstrated by women during birth. Often, just her calm presence is all that is required, to signal unobtrusively that all is proceeding well. Women in labour rarely need more than a few well chosen words to establish the feeling of labouring well. Creating this relationship requires midwives to harmonise with women and to follow their cues.

In general, women do not need "rescuing" from their labour. The birth process might be hard and sometimes painful work, but it is well within the scope of women to master it and to give birth successfully. Indeed, having the opportunity to experience labour, with all of its force and majesty might be an essential factor in enabling women to discover their inner strengths. Denying them this chance to find their own resources and prove their own worth as creative beings may undermine confidence, especially in innate nurturing abilities.

The drive to protect one's baby is so strong that women will generally give their all to ensure the safety of their child. This may be particularly important during labour, which, because of its inherent unknown quantity, appears to be particularly dangerous. Women go to extraordinary lengths to nurture their babies during the pregnancy, and will endure much to ensure the safe arrival of the infant. If we accidentally take over a woman's labour, it could be inter-

27

preted as proof of our belief that she does not have what it takes to nurture and protect her child. The sense of achievement and satisfaction experienced by women following undisturbed births attests to the confidence-building nature of the process. We must be very careful that we do not unintentionally undermine this important opportunity for personal growth — the self esteem of the new mother might be at stake.

Health professionals must be particularly sensitive to this issue. Rescue efforts are the hallmark of the medical model, where they are entirely necessary and appropriate. Birth, sitting as it does, in the social realm, does not require the same approach, and indeed, may be damaged by a zealous need to save women from pain and effort. In making the changeover from nursing to midwifery, many midwives have understood this important point, and have been able to abandon their enthusiastic helping strategies in favour of a more reasoned, intuitive approach. There are, however, many midwives who still persist in treating women as patients, in need of care and medical assistance (usually in the form of pain killing drugs) and these midwives would benefit from examining their motives and re-learning midwifery skills.

The biggest influence on attitudes to birth is probably personal experience. We were all born once, and we will have deep-seated memories of the event. Although buried under heavy layers of experiences from later life, these memories may still emerge from the unconscious, perhaps during times of acute stress. Giving birth to one's own children will have added further memories that will never be forgotten. Spending time with women as they give birth, especially when responsible for their care, creates another layer of powerful impressions. Stories shared amongst women about birth and parenting are another influence. Taken together, we all have strong views and perceptions about birth, all of it very personal and not necessarily applicable to others. These beliefs and attitudes will affect the way we behave around labouring women, and influence our views on the inherent safety of birth. For midwives, taking a close look at these personal views, and assessing their impact on professional performance is an essential part of developing good practice. Once you know where your beliefs are based, it is easier to understand your approach to birth and labouring women.

Having explored some of the general influences affecting midwives and their relationships with women, how can midwives effectively tune in to women's needs during pregnancy and birth? Whilst some midwives may have a natural talent for establishing empathy, skills for developing warmth and trust can be acquired and nurtured. All midwifery courses would benefit from the inclusion of extensive, practical training in basic skills possessed by counsellors. Since birth is largely a social event, social skills are of primary importance. If birth was a medical event, then much attention would need to be paid to medical management; the fact that few midwifery courses include competency in basic communication skills, problem solving and social support strategies as basic learner outcomes for their students reflects the medicalisation of birth and birth professionals.

Simple skills in listening, reflecting, paraphrasing and reframing would enable midwives to improve the quality of their communications with women and avoid misunderstandings. Cultural differences would be better accommodated because there would be a higher level of acceptance developed through better insight into personal needs. Protection of a woman's rights can be initiated and improved when her wishes are better understood, and this is more likely to happen as a result of careful listening and recognition of her position. The skills required to do this are beyond the scope of this book and in any case competency can only be gained through practical training. There are many courses available that midwives can utilise if it has not been included in their midwifery training: evening classes, weekend courses and even books, such as *Basic Personal Counselling* (Geldard 1993) can help you gain the basic skills.

Another step in developing rapport is to pay attention to your own personal style of communication and interaction. Developing the ability to assess yourself as others perceive you can be very illuminating and help you gain insights into ways of improving your relationships with women. This was discussed in the previous chapter.

Establishing rapport with others is often unconsciously achieved. Non-verbal signals and responses automatically show that a connection has been made: try watching two people in a deep conversation. Their bodies move forward and backward as though they are dancing together, and their heads and hands mirror each other's gestures. Even their legs may be crossed and uncrossed as though in harmony, yet all these actions take place apparently automatically.

Knowing how rapport is signalled unconsciously show us ways of connecting with women in particular situations. Midwives often find that they are caring for a woman whom they have never met before, and about whom they know very little. Trying to establish trust and a mutually agreeable working relationship can be difficult with people you don't know and it can take time, which may not be available. The changing of shifts, when a new team arrives to take on the care during labour is another tricky time. How can you quickly make yourself known, yet avoid disturbing the atmosphere surrounding the birth? It is very easy to disrupt women in labour unintentionally, and each time this happens, there is a risk that the labour will slow down until the mood can be recreated.

Some suggestions for achieving rapport:

➡ Initially, stand back a little and survey the whole scene: look at where people are located, what is happening, how they are interacting. Check the mood and general ambience. Note the level of conversation, its tone, volume and amount. Observe where the woman has positioned herself, her movements and reactions to contractions.

➡ Next, make whatever observations of the labour you can, while maintaining your distance. If you need to know about the quality and frequency of the contractions, for example, a few minutes of quiet observation will give you the answers, without the need to ask the woman, or her partner, directly.

➡ When you approach the woman, position yourself at her level. Avoid standing over her or in front of her. It is likely that she will have her eyes closed, as she concentrates on what is happening inside her body. Standing beside rather than facing her will reduce the risk of her opening her eyes — when someone faces you, you are likely to make eye contact and this is a powerful distraction for a labouring woman. Positioning yourself shoulder to shoulder will still enable you to observe from the corner of your eyes, and be less confronting.

➡ Imitate some of her behaviours, and take your cues from her. If she is quiet, avoid asking questions. If she has her head down and is resting, whisper in her ear. To let her know you are there, place your hand gently on her arm or shoulder, rather than speaking to announce your presence.

➡ If you need to check the baby's heartbeat, do so as unobtrusively as possible, and try to move her as little as possible. Having to move every half hour for this kind of check can break the rhythm of her labour. Further pointers on assessing progress in labour are included in Chapter 6.

Ideally, she should be aware of your presence, but only as a sensation or feeling. Direct interaction, discussion, asking questions and making eye contact are all to be avoided. Your aim is to leave her in charge of her labour, in an undisturbed place that evokes feelings of privacy, intimacy and safety. Women who labour like this are more likely to feel that they have given birth, using their own resources, rather than been delivered of a baby following the midwife's directions. If you can get into deep rapport with the woman, she may not even acknowledge your contribution — it is as if you have become an extension of herself, another of her own internal resources. This has to be the ultimate accolade of your ability to get in tune with women! The woman who says "I couldn't have done it without you" may be reflecting her feeling that you were the strong, permission-giving person who enabled her to find her own strengths, or she may be reflecting the feeling that without your direction and control over her, she would have never have known how to get the baby born. How would you like women to feel about their abilities after giving birth?

Women you don't like

Personality clashes are a part of life. With so many different types of people around, it is inevitable that from time to time, you will meet someone, or need to work with someone whom you don't particularly like. You may have different backgrounds, cultural beliefs, or personal idiosyncrasies that don't mesh comfortably. Therefore, sometimes you will find that you are caring for a woman in labour who you just don't like. If you are unable to find someone else to attend to her in labour, you will need to find ways of getting in tune with her needs, and providing professional companionship. One way of doing this is to consciously use the techniques described above to establish a good working relationship. When we like someone it is simple to forge an easy camaraderie — when we don't automatically "click", we can still maintain our professional approach by signalling our availability and attention through mirroring some of her behaviours. You may need to do this in a very conscious way, and if you do it well, paying particular attention to your nonverbal as well as verbal responses, she should never know that you do not particularly like her as a person. It could be said that establishing rapport with people you like is easy, while being able to achieve the same outcome with people you don't like is one hallmark of a truly professional person.

Women who are in a panic

The scenario is familiar to most midwives: the woman arrives in the labour ward, yelling for help, complaining, moving around wildly, experiencing excruciatingly painful contractions. The initial impression is that perhaps she is in transition, yet somehow this doesn't feel right. Eventually, an internal examination shows that she is 3 centimetres dilated. This woman is not in transition, she is in a panic. Another example: the woman appears to be labouring well, with long hard contractions, yet is not dilating. Her eyes are searching wildly for help, she is expressing fear of being able to make it without pain killing drugs, and she is having difficulty getting comfortable. This woman is also panicking, and she too, needs your help.

These scenarios are common in hospitals, where the environment, both physical and human, is not always conducive to peaceful, productive labour. Learning how to calm people who are panicking would be a very useful addition to basic training since this is a situation that midwives will have to deal with frequently.

Dealing with their own panic is beyond parents themselves. Teaching the woman or her partner ways of managing their own fearfulness are probably a waste of time, and may actually be harmful, since this approach creates the impression that panic is normal and to be expected. The difference between the out-of-control feelings of transition, and panic at other times needs, however, to be understood, particularly by caregivers. Being able to tell the difference and act accordingly is an important skill for midwives, since the "panicky" behaviours associated with transition are normal, and not a problem, but signs of panic at other times are indicative of distress that needs attention. Signs of panic:

- restlessness, moving around
- wide open eyes
- loud voice, shouting, screaming, yelling
- raised blood pressure
- voicing of fear and anxiety
- generalised agitation.

Once again, there is a need to establish rapport with this woman, so that she can be calmed and her adrenalin level can fall, thus enabling a resumption of the natural flow of oxytocin and endorphins. The same techniques as before can be used, although this time, instead of quietening down your behaviour, you may need to liven it up. If she is making a lot of noise, then you will need to raise your voice. If her eyes are wide open and staring, then make strong eye contact with her and become her centre of focus. If she is moving around, move with her, keeping up the pace. These actions will register your attention and concern for her and let her know that you are in harmony with her, even in her distress. If you act quietly, and try to calm her through soothing words from the start, she may not even notice your presence.

Once you have her attention, and she recognises that you are there to help (she is usually calling out for assistance) then you can gradually slow down your own movements, drop the volume of your voice, lower it in pitch and breathe more slowly. She will respond, especially if you make strong eye contact, and perhaps even hold her protectively at the same time. As her distress subsides, you can help her to slow down her breathing and sink into a resting posture. You can then gradually withdraw your close contact. Once she begins to calm down, encouraging her to take a shower or bath may help remove the last traces of adrenalin while affording her the privacy she needs to get back in touch with her labour.

It may take some time to completely settle her, and you should take this into account before further assessing the progress of her labour. When she is calm, you can make some appropriate suggestions, or answer her questions. It might be helpful to tell her that as the labour picks up again, she will begin to produce endorphins that will help her into a dreamy, trance like state. As this happens the labour will feel much better and more manageable.

A woman who has been in any kind of panic needs calm people around her, then positive input and generous encouragement. A final step might be some time on her own in private to get back into equilibrium.

Supporting autonomy and discouraging dependence

Many women, particularly when they arrive into a hospital, become very dependent. The hospital setting itself sends out strong signals that dependency is expected: beds, hospital clothing, wrist tags, medicinal smells, medical equipment, clinical decor and strangers all create a feeling that inmates should be quiet, well-behaved, compliant, obedient and above all, trustful that others know what is best for them and their baby.

In addition, not all women are used to being in positions of power, and not all are good at making decisions or solving problems. The unknown routines of what is so obviously an important workplace for a large number of highly trained people is at best daunting, and commonly totally overwhelming. It is no wonder that women generally feel insecure and dependent in these surroundings. There would be relatively few women who could take charge in this setting and maintain their autonomy. Most women will therefore lapse into dependent behaviour — even finding the toilet on their own may be difficult. Becoming instinctive and losing one's inhibitions may be impossible.

Women will generally seek guidance. They don't want to look silly, and they want to be seen as "good patients". Some parts of labour can be especially embarrassing, and having to use the toilet, vomit or pass wind can lead to feelings of humiliation. Oxytocin is easily inhibited by feelings of embarrassment, and many women will find their labours slow and unproductive in these circumstances. The impression that you create, as the midwife, can have a significant impact on the woman in labour: you can enable her to maintain her autonomy and authority, to exercise her independence and instincts, her belief in her innate resources and natural responses. Alternatively, you could help her become a compliant, subservient patient, leaning on you for guidance and assistance, looking to you for advice and reassurance, requesting instruction and taking orders. You could leave her in the "box seat" or you could take over and manage the labour yourself.

The advantages of maintaining the woman's central position during birth have already been outlined. This would be the goal of most midwives, yet frequently, the opposite happens, and the midwife finds herself inadvertently in charge. What can you do to maintain the woman's autonomy and independence?

➡ Arrange for her to visit your unit in advance so that she can become more familiar with its layout and function. Ways of making this more effective are discussed in Chapter 7.

➡ Encourage her to bring parts of her "nest" from home. Her own pillows, bedspread or duvet, clothes, pictures, flowers, aromatic oils, food, drink and similar items will all help soften the clinical appearance of the labour room.

➡ Encourage her to bring companions to share her journey through birth. These should be people of her own choosing and invitation. Being surrounded by significant others can make her feel more secure and they can provide a buffer between her and the outside world. Ways of choosing and using birth companions are described in Chapter 7.

➡ Remember that hospital protocols are only guidelines. You can vary them if the situation warrants it — you may need to get permission, and you must document what you have done and why. This is discussed in greater detail in Chapter 8.

➡ Encourage problem solving behaviour in labour. For example, if she says her back is aching, rather than telling her to learn forward and instructing her partner to rub her back, you could say "some women find leaning forward helps — how about trying to find a way to do this while I go and get some extra pillows for you?". Giving the woman a chance to work out a solution on her own, with no professionals watching, can be helpful.

➡ Try to be as unobtrusive as possible. She will sense your presence, and there is no need to loudly announce your arrival or fuss about, drawing attention to your needs as a midwife. If you keep a low profile, she will not feel obliged to respond to *you*, or to accommodate *your* wishes, when she really needs to focus on herself.

In addition to the points outlined above, be aware of those particularly critical times during labour when she is especially sensitive to her surroundings and the people with her. Arriving at the hospital, in labour, is one such time. The "ground rules" and functional parameters of the labour ward are conveyed through a series of messages many of which are subtle and the woman may record subconsciously:

- the smell
- the clinical appearance
- the presence, amount and arrangement of the equipment
- the furniture, which will be different from what she is used to
- noises, especially those coming from women in labour in nearby rooms
- staff conversation and non-verbal messages
- the public nature of the area and its business
- posters or signs, and so on …

How can you create a warm, accepting, open, friendly and woman centred impression? Try imagining a typical admission sequence in your hospital. Picture the couple arriving in your unit and what happens to them. When you go to meet them you will no doubt greet them warmly, with a friendly smile and welcoming manner. You will probably usher her and her companion(s) to a place where you can talk and check her progress. What will this room be like? Perhaps it is a small assessment room, used solely for these admission procedures. In some hospitals, the woman is shown directly into the room where she will labour and give birth. In other places, she may be admitted to a shared room, where other women may be waiting or even in labour.

Where will you invite her to settle? Will you offer her (and her partner) a chair, or will you indicate the bed? Sometimes, the bed is the only place for her to sit. In practice is seems that women usually gravitate there, either automatically or at the midwife's invitation. Of course, women have been well conditioned to getting on the bed — all her pre-natal visits will have involved some time lying down while being checked. She will be familiar with lying down in the presence of health professionals, and will have learned that it is expected behaviour. What kind of message has she received from this? What are we telling her: that midwives are very accommodating as a rule, but when certain "midwifery" tasks are required they must take place on the bed? That she can labour anywhere she likes as long as she gets onto the bed for the serious procedures (such as the birth itself)? Midwives often say that they enjoy assisting women give birth on the floor, yet women keep getting onto the beds — very frustrating for the adventurous and sensitive midwife! Perhaps if we looked at how women are conditioned during pregnancy we might find some clues as to why this occurs.

What would happen if instead, we asked her to sit in a chair? Now she is upright, less subservient, more able to take charge. The unspoken, and often unintended, power play ("I'm in charge here!") is less defined when she is able to make more direct eye contact with you, especially if you, too, are seated. Standing over a woman and looking down at her gives a strong signal about you and your position and status, and is a message about her role —

35

"you are a patient now, so be good and do as you are told". Of course, this may not be your intention at all, but you may have accidentally undermined her confidence and removed her autonomy all the same.

Another way of encouraging this scenario is to make it clear that the bed has other uses. Imagine meeting her at the door, relieving her or her partner of some of her belongings and then as you enter the room, heading for the bed, where you place her things in the middle. There is no way she will want to sit on the bed now! You can casually pull up three chairs (or unstack them from the corner) and offer them around, all the while chatting on in a friendly manner. Once you are all seated, you can continue with your assessment. Everyone is on the same level, everyone is equal, everyone can behave as a responsible adult. Your assessment can mostly be done while she is seated, and ways of doing this are described in Chapter 6.

Another area requiring particular sensitivity involves working with women who have suffered some form of sexual, emotional or psychological abuse in the past. It will not always be possible to identify these women in advance, although some of their behaviours might suggest this unfortunate history. Many of the procedures involved with birth are potentially hazardous for these women, and run the risk of evoking fear and severe anxiety. Even something as simple as lying down, with a stranger standing over her may be too much for some women, and internal examinations, unpleasant for all women, are often unbearably painful (physically and emotionally) for some. This is one aspect of maternity where continuity of carer can pay particular dividends, since it is more likely that the midwife will have been able to discuss past history. When you find yourself caring for women you have never met, it is usually impossible to know about their previous life experiences — perhaps the best way to proceed is as if all women in your care may be potential victims, and avoid any situations that may be interpreted as potentially threatening. Hospital protocols that require regular internal examinations, for example, need to be re-written, to enable midwives to freely exercise their professional judgement about their necessity. Reducing trauma for labouring women is a powerful argument for avoiding all these kinds of routine procedures.

There are further simple strategies in Chapter 6 that you can use to implement and reinforce women's autonomy. All of them require forethought and sometimes, conscious action. Using them and paying attention to their impact is a way of demonstrating your willingness and ability in establishing and maintaining close professional interactions with women based on their needs, not yours. A caring, sensitive midwife is characterised by a natural easiness and obvious comfort with other women. She shows insight, perception and is unobtrusive, especially when performing tasks that might create anxiety or disturb a woman's labour. These are skills, however, that midwives can learn.

References

Geldard D. 1993, *Basic Personal Counselling*, Prentice Hall, Australia.

Chapter 5

THE PHYSIOLOGY OF LABOUR AND BIRTH

Before we can begin to explore practical measures for self-help in labour we need to examine the basic biological mechanisms that control the process. Safety is the key issue, for survival of the species depends not only on producing a healthy baby, but on ensuring that the baby's arrival into the world is as untraumatic as possible. In addition, giving birth must not only be physically possible for a woman to achieve, but innately rewarding, so that she is encouraged to reproduce again.

The following descriptions of the basic hormonal interactions in labour have been adapted from my earlier book *Empowering Women — teaching active birth in the 90s*. In that context the information was intended for use by childbirth educators as a basis for their work in educating women. Here the aim is to remind midwives of those simple physiological facts that have tended to become lost amongst the plethora of technological inventions that have been introduced to control rather than promote normal labour.

When we are born, we arrive in the world equipped with innate and instinctive behaviours designed to ensure that we survive, eventually reproduce and therefore perpetuate our species. The controlling centres for these essential behaviours are in the hypothalamic region of the brain, often called "the ancient brain", and the instincts involved are implanted there very early in fetal life. Most of the time, the circumstances that fire off the "flight or fight" mechanisms of survival are quite separate from those that encourage us to reproduce. During labour and birth, the two areas become interconnected since the mother, while using her reproductive instincts is very vulnerable to attack and a successful outcome will depend on her being protected from potentially life threatening situations. Should such a threat arise, nature instigates a series of life-preserving reactions designed to increase the chances of survival. It is the interplay of the mechanisms for survival and reproduction that shapes much of the physiology of labour and birth.

These mechanisms are governed by several hormones in a complex and inter-related ways. The main hormonal players in these events are oxytocin, endorphins and the catecholamines (adrenalin). We cannot physically control their release and turn them on and off at will. They are secreted automatically resulting in instinctive reactions and innate responses.

The flow of labour is controlled by oxytocin. This hormone is sensitive to adrenalin, which drives the survival behaviours. The role of the endorphins is to protect the mother during labour from excessive pain, to raise her sensitivity to her body's needs and to enable her to labour more effectively.

Before discussing the effects of endorphin and adrenaline on the contractions, we must understand how the contractions are stimulated, and the underlying physical processes of birth. Oxytocin in the major hormone involved in driving the uterus to contract.

Oxytocin

Oxytocin has often been called "the hormone of love", as it is the key hormone governing all aspects of reproductive behaviours in both men and women. It is produced in the hypothalamic region of the brain and is stored and secreted by the posterior pituitary gland. Ultimately, oxytocin release is controlled by the brain, therefore its release can be influenced by other cortical activities, including operant conditioning.

Ferguson first described, in 1941, the reflex whereby oxytocin is released from the posterior pituitary gland in response to stimulation of certain sites involved in reproduction, such as the vagina, clitoris, cervix and the nipples. When oxytocin is released as a result of stimulation of these areas it has a number of effects:

- Its presence triggers caretaking behaviours: males become more protective of females and in return, females provide comfort and support for males. This closeness may be an important mechanism for ensuring that offspring have two parents.

- The manufacture of sperm in enhanced and early ovulation in females is encouraged.

- The motility of the fallopian tubes increases which influences sperm transport during sexual intercourse.
- Sperm transport is also assisted by the "in-sucking" action of the uterus when it contracts.
- Following orgasm, anxiety states and depression are reduced. Orgasm makes you feel better!
- Skin temperature is affected — the body and particularly the breasts become warmer.
- During pregnancy, the "in-sucking" action of the cervix keeps it tightly closed, thus maintaining the pregnancy. The precise trigger for the reversal of the action, necessary to initiate labour, has not yet been determined.
- The continual, mild contractions of the pregnant uterus keeps the muscle well-toned and assists in maintaining a good blood flow to the placenta.
- It causes the uterus to contract during birth, pressing the baby against cervix, which stimulates further contractions thus maintaining the progress of the labour.
- Distension of the vagina and pelvic floor muscles as the baby descends continues the release of oxytocin, which causes the longitudinal muscle fibres in the uterus to push down on the baby. In this way, the baby's descent is almost a "closed loop" of reflex action and is an important "fail safe" mechanism to ensure that the baby can be born, without maternal effort if necessary.
- As the baby crowns, the stretching of the perineal tissues initiates another surge of oxytocin, to begin the separation of the placenta and to ready colostrum in the breasts, to attract the baby.
- It initiates the milk ejection reflex, which is a basic component of the milk supply system for the newborn.
- Oxytocin release during lactation has been shown to induce maternal, nurturing behaviours.
- It causes strong contractions of the uterus during breastfeeding thus aiding its return to a pre-pregnant condition.
- During orgasm or masturbation it can cause a lactating female to release her milk.

These are some of the broad effects of oxytocin release across a range of reproductive behaviours. Although it has wide functions in every aspect of the sexual cycle, it is its action during labour that is our particular concern, and therefore we must examine its role in labour more closely.

Once labour has begun, the ebb and flow of oxytocin shapes the pattern of the contractions. The hormone is released as a result of pressure from the presenting part of the baby against the cervix. If the head becomes well applied, the contractions become regular and consistent. If the baby is breech, the soft buttocks may exert a less even pressure, leading to irregular, less powerful contractions. A baby presenting in a posterior position, with a deflexed head, will exert pressures on the pelvic bones, especially the sacral area of the pelvic brim rather than the cervix, and many of these labours start very slowly, with much backache and inconsistent contractions.

Whilst the membranes remain intact, the pressure of the head against the cervix will be cushioned by the bag of forewaters. With a well positioned head, this pressure will be transferred effectively through the intact membranes and the contractions will be efficient, whilst the baby's head will be protected from undue direct pressure.

If the membranes are ruptured artificially once labour has started, the removal of this cushioning bag of forewaters will cause the baby's head to press directly on the cervix. This may result in sudden stimulation and strong, powerful contractions for both mother and baby. Fetal distress may be triggered by the increased compression of the baby's head, and the mother may request pain relief since her endorphin level may not yet be high enough to compensate for the increased pain.

The last few centimetres of dilatation are usually referred to as the "transition" phase of labour. The uterine contractions begin to change their effect, from pulling the cervix open, to pushing the baby down through the birth canal. The amniotic sac frequently ruptures at this time as a result of extra pressure on the membranes. This, in turn, leads to sustained contractions useful in achieving the final centimetres of dilatation. These heavier contractions, and the resultant pain, causes endorphin levels to rise in response. If the membranes are still intact, the forewaters may bulge through the cervix, initiating an early desire the push even though the cervix may not be fully dilated.

There may be a lull between first and second stage when dilatation is complete, yet the baby has not begun its descent which triggers the next phase of oxytocin production. As a result, the contractions may cease, and the mother and baby may gain a welcome rest period. Once the head does begin to descend, oxytocin is released in response to the opening out of the pelvic floor muscles as the head passes through, together with distension of the vagina.

When the baby's head reaches the perineum, there is a further stretching of muscle and tissue prior to crowning. Once again, there is a surge of oxytocin in response to this stretching, to maintain the woman's pushing urge and to ensure there is oxytocin in her body for a short period after the birth. It is thought that the release of oxytocin at this point may also ready colostrum in the breasts, to encourage the baby to find the nipple.

After the baby is born, the uterus continues to contract to assist the placenta to separate and be expelled. This task is aided by another flow of oxytocin, this time as a result of nipple stimulation. The nipples are very sensitive immediately after birth and any touch of the baby's mouth or tongue will be registered. Usually, with an hour of the birth the baby will begin to suckle, but even the preparatory nuzzling and licking can stimulate oxytocin release in the woman's body. Once the baby latches to the nipple and begin to suck, there is a powerful surge of oxytocin, necessary for the expulsion of the placenta and the avoidance of haemorrhage. The amount of oxytocin released at this time is probably greater than at any other time during the labour.

As well as assisting in the completion of third stage and preventing bleeding, the rush of oxytocin raises her skin temperature, so that the baby stays warm when nestled against her, skin to skin. She is also flooded with nurturing feelings for the baby. Thus oxytocin becomes an important element in the initial attachment process between mother and baby.

Much of the analysis and identification of the actions of oxytocin was completed by early lactational physiologists such as Niles Newton (1971, 1978). Newton was the first to describe the "fetus ejection reflex" (Newton 1966, 1987) in which the body produces a surge of oxytocin in response to extreme fear at critical times during birth. There is more about this interesting phenomenon at the end of this chapter. To summarise the effects of oxytocin:

Ways of stimulating oxytocin production

- Distension of the vagina
- Clitoral stimulation
- Pressure on the cervix
- Distension of the pelvic floor muscles
- Stretching of the perineum
- Nipple stimulation
- Conditioned reflexes

Factors which inhibit oxytocin production

Direct

- Fear or anxiety caused by:

  external factors — being moved during labour, unpleasant smell, strange people, noise, distractions, bright lights, feeling exposed etc.

  Internal factors — concerns about the baby's health, worry about perineal tearing, fear of pain etc.

- Anaesthetic injections (epidural, pudendal blocks, local anaesthetics), which numb the nerves at the receptor sites necessary for the initiation of the Ferguson Reflex.
- Induction and augmentation, which flood the receptor sites with abnormally high levels of oxytocin, rendering them less sensitive to the physiologic doses produced in the body.
- Episiotomy, which reduces the stretching of the perineum, thus removing one triggering factor for oxytocin release.
- Separation of mother and baby at birth, leading to a lack of nipple stimulation necessary for maintaining oxytocin flow during the third stage of labour.

Indirect

- Beliefs and attitudes, which may lead to embarrassment, a powerful inhibitor of oxytocin.
- Memories, perhaps of past sexual abuse, which may remain subconscious (leading to an unexplained discomfort) or become conscious (leading to fear).
- Embarrassment or anger.

Results of oxytocin inhibition

- Failure to achieve orgasm — perhaps leading to difficulties in long term relationships due to lack of oxytocin-initiated nurturing and caretaking behaviours between partners
- Slowing of labour — contractions are further apart
- Slower dilation due to contractions of reduced strength
- Prolonged second stage of labour — due to little or no urge to push
- Increased likelihood of post-partum haemorrhage following birth
- Problems with breastfeeding due to a faulty milk ejection reflex.

Endorphins

Endorphins are natural substances similar to opiates in structure that are produced in the brain stem, nerve endings, and even the placenta. They appear whenever the body is physically stressed beyond its normal limits. A common example of endorphin release, and one familiar to most people, is the "jogger's high" that runners experience when pushing themselves beyond their normal physical limits. At this point the runner's body releases a surge of endorphins and the jogger gets his "second wind" which enables him to keep on running.

There are three main effects of endorphins: they modify pain, create a sense of well-being, and alter perception of time and place. The behavioural effects of endorphins are quite noticeable, and in labouring women are particularly helpful in assessing their progress. Their presence can also be used diagnostically, as a measure of the normalcy of the labour.

The presence of endorphins enables a balance to be struck between the need for pain in labour and the desirability of encouraging the woman to reproduce again. If the pain is overwhelming and disproportionate to the rewards, then further pregnancies will be avoided. If, on the other hand, the labour is manageable (even satisfying), then giving birth will not seem such a terrifying prospect, and the species will have a better hope of survival. The fact that the human race has been so successful in populating the earth suggests that the mechanism works, given opportunity.

Understanding the need for pain in labour

The main symptoms of labour are painful contractions of the uterus. Very few women labour without some degree of pain, therefore this universal experience must have a biological purpose and an integral role in the reproductive process. It seems likely that there are two main reasons for the presence of some pain during birth — one physical, the other psychological.

The first concerns the need for a woman to know she is in labour and how far she has progressed, so she can judge the arrival time of the baby. This is important if she is to find a safe place in which to give birth. All animals either prepare or identify a special area to which they retreat when they sense that birth is imminent. In addition, it is interesting to note that nocturnal animals give birth during the day and diurnal animals at night — a mechanism designed to ensure privacy from other members of the species and to reduce the danger from natural predators.

Contractions also have a specific character according to the stage of labour and this provides the biofeedback mechanism that lets a woman judge her progress. The twinges and sporadic contractions of early labour announce the beginning of the labour whilst the unmistakably powerful contractions of transition indicate that the labour is nearing its conclusion. Pushing contractions in second stage are reliable signs of imminent birth. At each stage a woman reacts differently to these stimuli and an experienced midwife can often tell from observation of the woman's reactions to her contractions, the rate of dilatation of the cervix, without the need for invasive internal examinations.

Women who have painless labours or precipitate births often find these very unpleasant and even frightening experiences. Perhaps the signals of an impending birth (usually transition contractions) trigger innate fears for the safety of the baby, should it arrive before the chosen birth place can be reached. In addition, there is little time for her to adjust to her labour either physically (through endorphin release) or emotionally and this can lead to a state of shock which may take some time to resolve.

The psychological advantages of experiencing pain in labour have often been mentioned by women. Accepting the powerful sensations created by the labouring uterus and riding with strong and sometimes painful contractions to produce the miracle of a baby, offers women unique opportunities for self-discovery and growth through mastery of this potentially life threatening situation. Submission to the all-consuming and overwhelming nature of birth and the weathering of the inherent pain of labour is an empowering process for a woman, and one which she should not be denied unless critical for her own well-being or that of her baby.

The basic pain messages received by the brain during labour stem from the stimulation of sensory nerves in the uterine muscle mass. The uterus contains only sensory nerve endings that register sensations caused by stretching and tearing. There are no specialised nerve endings that react to other stimuli such as cutting, application of heat, cold, pressure etc. Therefore the primary source of pain is the stretching of the cervix. The need for a clear signal in the unlikely event of the tearing of the uterus is obvious as this is a life threatening situation for the woman and her baby.

Other abdominal organs and tissues surrounding the uterus have additional sensory nerve fibres and may register a variety of sensations: pressure from the uterus and baby as the labour advances; pressure on a full bladder or bowel; pain from compression of nerves and bones caused by the position of the baby's head, etc. These additional discomforts can often be eased, and are peripheral to the pain of the actual birth process.

As labour gathers strength the nature of the contractions change and the amount of pain registered by the woman increases, providing a mechanism for assessing progress in labour. As the end of first stage nears, the contractions become very intense, closer together and much more painful. The mother enters the transition phase between first and second stage and involuntary changes in her behaviour occur. The pain is stronger because the contractions are longer and a greater stretch is being exerted on the cervix to open it the last few centimetres. Once the cervix is fully open, the baby begins to descend through the birth canal, and the sensations again change in nature. Pain is no longer initiated by the stretching cervix as this is fully open, but the woman may register pressure on tissues surrounding the vagina, or on the pelvic bones, if the baby is a tight fit.

If the cervix opens unevenly, cervical pain may still be felt even though the woman is apparently into second stage, indicated by her desire to push. If a woman finds pushing painful, especially if there are no signs of descent, the cervix may have dilated unevenly with an anterior lip that may be impeding progress. Appropriate measures must be taken to reduce pressure from the baby on this lip of cervix until it is fully retracted (this is best achieved by the mother assuming a knee-chest position). Pain with pushing urges is a powerful disincentive for a labouring woman and she will try to hold back and reduce her effort to protect herself from damaging the cervix.

In early second stage (the latent phase) the contractions can be mild, with few pushing urges. There may even be a complete break, allowing time for mother and baby to rest before beginning the work of birth. This rest period is more common in primiparous women. As momentum builds up, the pushing urges become more organised as the uterus undertakes the expulsion of the baby. As the baby descends through the birth canal, the pelvic floor muscles open out and the vagina unfolds to accommodate the baby on its journey towards birth. Pain from the stretching of the cervix is absent, but the opening of the pelvic floor muscles could be painful, unless they are completely relaxed. The vagina is capacious and unfolds easily. When the baby's head reaches the perineal tissues, they begin to stretch slowly. This causes the stinging 'rim of fire' sensation that heralds the baby's imminent arrival, usually passing in minutes as the baby's head crowns and is born. This sudden burning pain encourages the woman to once again hold back from pushing too hard and is another example of a biofeedback system designed to prevent damage to the woman's reproductive organs (in this case, the perineum).

These sources of pain are normally present in labour, and form an integral part of the process. The amount of pain a woman will register is modified by many factors, some physical and others psychological. Pain will be increased if a woman is frightened or anxious during labour, if she assumes uncomfortable positions (which place undue pressure on surrounding structures and tissues), if her baby is malpositioned (for example, presenting in the occipito-posterior position), or if there is some other mechanical problem such as cephalopelvic disproportion or a full bowel or bladder obstructing progress.

Such messages of extreme pain are diagnostic and encourage a woman to seek remedies to reduce the physical causes of her pain. Severe pain in second stage can indicate a tight fit between the baby and the pelvic bones, with extra pressure being felt on the sacrum or ischial spines. This situation is exacerbated by unphysiologic positions for birth, particularly semi-sitting, and a change of position may relieve the pain. Touching the perineum in second stage is also painful for the mother and should be avoided by caregivers.

That pain has an essential role in labour is acknowledged by the body's ability to produce its own pain modifying substances — endorphins — to assist women through the rigours of labour.

Assessing endorphin levels

In pregnancy, a woman's body undergoes a natural state of stress as it copes with the extra workload due to the requirements of the developing baby. As the months pass, the level of endorphins gradually rises in response to this stress, and towards the end of pregnancy, she will have constantly raised levels in her system. Many women report behavioural effects during the last few weeks of the pregnancy probably attributable to these increased endorphin levels: a feeling of well-being, of acceptance and readiness for the baby; broken sleep with a tendency to lie awake for hours; vivid dreams; noticeable maternal amnesia, for example. They are reassuring signs that her system is already producing endorphins and that it will continue to do so, especially once she is in labour.

Once labour begins in earnest, the endorphin level continues to rise. After some time in "pre-labour" the contractions begin to strengthen, to a point where they are measurably stronger, requiring concentration. Around this time, a woman begins to physically slow down to focus more directly on what is happening. It will be observed that the contractions are coming more regularly and somewhat closer together. This increase in tempo of the labour stimulates endorphin production, and its release is heralded by her change in behaviour: she becomes withdrawn; more sedentary; rests between contractions; closes her eyes; and appears "spaced out". These signs are all proof that her endorphin levels are adequate for her needs and that the labour is progressing normally. It is at this point that labour would be described as "established".

During the transition phase of labour, there is a physical upheaval as the uterus changes its action from opening the cervix to pushing the baby out. The contractions become quite painful, are closer together, and seem unremitting in their intensity. Endorphin production is at its highest at this point, assisting the woman to manage the pain, but also enabling her to focus inwardly. Many women become quite disoriented and the accompanying amnesic effect means that she may have difficulty remembering much of the detail of this part of labour after the baby is born.

Transition is often the point where women are suddenly confronted by overwhelming fears that they are unable to complete the birth, that they cannot cope and that, in extreme circumstances, they might die. It may be that the high levels of endorphin produce these hallucinations, and that overcoming this confrontation with life and death is important to the subsequent feeling of achievement reported by many women after birth. Little is known about the psychological effects of endorphins in labour, but their presence in normal labour probably serves an important psychological as well as physical purpose.

Once transition passes the contractions usually slow, become shorter and may even stop for a time. The high levels of endorphins engendered by the powerful transition contractions create a feeling of well being and help a woman to get her second wind. Even women who have had very long and arduous labours can experience this surge of energy at the beginning of second stage.

During second stage, endorphin levels remain high in response to the work of pushing. As soon as the baby is born, the effort of labour ceases and the woman experiences the characteristic euphoric state of high endorphin levels. She is elated, feels a sense of achievement, and is in a positive and receptive state, important for greeting her new baby.

It may well be that one of the most important reasons for endorphin production during labour is to ensure this optimal physical and emotional state immediately after the birth. From the baby's perspective, it is important that its mother is alert, welcoming and intensely interested in nurturing and protecting her newborn. This is vital for the baby's survival immediately after the birth and for the development of close bonds of attachment. A mother in a euphoric state is likely to meet these needs of the baby, who in turn, displays behaviour designed to appeal and attract attention in a positive way. Post-birth elation due to endorphins will not be present unless they have been stimulated into production earlier in labour as a response to the contractions. Therefore, experiencing labour and its pain may be essential precursors for the bonding behaviours necessary for ensuring survival of the infant.

Following the birth, the endorphin level in the body falls dramatically, and about two days after the birth has returned almost to pre-pregnancy levels. The 'third day blues' that many women experience is thought to be a reaction to the sudden withdrawal of the endorphins she has had in her body (and to which she has become addicted) over the previous nine months. On the fourth or fifth day post-partum the levels of endorphin rise a little, and then gradually taper off, returning to pre-pregnant levels by around three weeks after the birth.

Catecholamines

When a person is frightened, fearful or in a potentially dangerous situation, the body automatically turns on survival behaviours, and releases hormones called catecholamines, commonly known as adrenalin and nor-adrenalin. These hormones are made in the brain, in the adrenal glands on top of the kidneys, in the nerve endings in the body, and in other locations. They act on nerve endings of the sympathetic nervous system, and produce what is commonly called the 'fight or flight' syndrome, a series of behaviours designed to effect a rescue from the source of danger.

We have probably all felt their effects at some time in our lives, and can recall a pounding heart, rapid breathing and a feeling of wanting to run away from the danger. Other symptoms are: an increase in blood sugar levels; a rise in blood pressure; a decrease of activity in the digestive system; a decrease of blood supply to the internal organs; cold clammy skin and dilated pupils. The net effect is that the body directs a flow of super oxygenated blood towards those parts of the body that are most useful in escaping from the danger — that is, the peripheral muscular system, the heart, the lungs, and the brain.

In labour, a woman finds that her body is subjected to a certain amount of stress, and as her labour builds in strength, she may breathe a little faster, her heart rate may increase and her blood pressure may rise slightly. These are all normal responses. If, however, she is subjected to additional distress from an external source that registers as an alarm, her body will automatically release adrenalin to assist her. Poor labour environments, frightening comments from carers, uncomfortable positions or an increase in pain that raises anxiety, could all have this effect. Now she is in a situation where her body has registered a threat. It is important to note that the source of the threat may be obvious (external) such as hearing forceps being discussed or noticing consultations with the doctor going on behind her back, or it could be a perceived threat such as the pervasive smell of hospitals reminding her of unpleasant past experiences. For some women the sense of threat may arise from psychological or emotional factors, for example, a fear that the baby will be handicapped, or when routine procedures trigger flashbacks of a sexual assault in the past.

In threatening circumstances, a woman feels a strong urge to seek safety for herself and her baby. The innate behaviours associated with survival and reproduction overlap at this point, therefore in addition to producing the usual survival mechanisms, reproductive behaviours must be slowed to avoid the baby arriving into a potentially dangerous situation. The release of adrenalin will be noticed by caregivers: she will be agitated and restless; be breathing rapidly; be making direct eye contact and have dilated pupils; be shivery or cold; have a raised blood pressure and a rapid pulse. As well, mechanisms to slow labour are initiated:

- The levels of oxytocin fall, in proportion to the amount of adrenalin in the system. This has the effect of slowing the contractions, perhaps causing them to stop altogether, particularly if there is little oxytocin being released, for example, in the early part of labour. Once labour has become established, with moderately high levels of oxytocin flowing, the contractions may slow in response to adrenalin, but are unlikely to stop altogether.

- To prevent further dilatation of the cervix, and perhaps the untimely birth of the baby, adrenalin stimulates the circular fibres in the lower third of the uterus to contract, to halt further dilatation. This action has an important side effects — once these circular fibres begin contracting, they work directly against the action of the longitudinal and figure-of-eight muscle fibres in the uterus, thus setting up a pattern of opposed muscle action. The resultant tug-of-war within the uterine muscle layers causes considerable pain, which may suggest that the contractions are working normally. Often, the combination of apparently strong contractions coupled with a lack of dilatation is labelled "failure to progress" or worse, "inco-ordinate uterine action", when in fact the phenomenon is a perfect example of the body's ability to respond normally in poor circumstances. Many women have had their uterus labelled as inefficient when in reality it was working perfectly. The additional pain from this opposed muscle contraction can be very intense and further add to a woman's fear, especially if she is told that these powerful contractions are not producing any dilatation. A request for pain relief is therefore likely.

- A further development of the normal action of adrenalin in re-organising the internal blood supply in frightening situations, is that the uterus finds itself contracting with reduced blood flow and therefore less oxygen. Contractions of the uterus, which is made up of smooth muscle fibres, are not normally painful, but if the blood flow is reduced, then the muscle will become ischaemic and therefore painful when contracting. This is similar to the contractions of the heart — these are not normally painful unless the blood supply is blocked, perhaps by occlusion of a coronary artery.

- The appearance of adrenalin in labour has an impact on endorphin levels. Endorphin levels fall in response to the flight/fight syndrome and will only reappear when the source of the disturbance is removed. Since it takes time for endorphin production to re-establish, allowance must be made for this to happen, and for the labour to gather pace once more. In practice, a woman may need an hour or more in the shower or bath, for

51

example, to reduce her adrenalin level sufficient for endorphin production to resume.

To summarise:

The clinical effects of adrenalin release in labour
- Panic behaviours:
  restlessness
  agitation
  loud noise — shouting, yelling
  wild movements
  activity
  wide, staring eyes
  raised blood pressure
- Slowing of contractions, perhaps cessation
- Increased pain during contractions
- A pause in dilatation — labour stalls with no further progress

Often diagnosed as
- "not in labour" — e.g. when the labour stops on arrival at the hospital
- "failure to progress"
- "arrested labour"
- "inco-ordinate uterine action"
- "dystocia"
- "inefficient myometrial activity"

More accurate diagnosis
- "A natural response to a threatening situation"
- "Normal rescue behaviours"
- "Perfect hormonal interplay given the circumstances"

Important points
- If the mother and baby show no signs of medical problems, there is no need to take medical action.
- Avoid using negative language and labels as they colour perceptions of the woman and her caregivers.
- Oxytocin drips should be used only as a last resort when everything has been tried and given time to work.

If it is impossible to provide a conducive environment or a feeling of safety and protection for the mother, she may need an epidural to compensate for her lack of endorphin and the resultant pain caused by the circumstances. The giving of epidurals should be regarded as an acknowledgment by the hospital and its staff of their failure to provide an appropriate labour environment, and not as a rescue remedy she automatically needs or deserves.

Some suggested courses of action are described in Chapter 6.

The role of the pelvis in labour

The bones of the pelvis are designed to provide protection and guidance for the baby as it is being born. The bony girdle is held together by a system of ligaments that soften during the pregnancy under the influence of the hormone relaxin. This increases the flexibility of the joints and enables women to significantly increase the space within the pelvic bones by altering their stance and body position.

Being upright enables the woman's legs to act as levers on the sides of the pelvis, which opens the outlet, making an easier passage for the baby. In this way she can create up to 28% more space (Russell 1982). In addition, the bones of the baby's skull are able to mould in response to a tight fit. Both of these mechanisms work to make the birth of the baby as safe as possible, and womens' preference for an upright stance demonstrates their instinctive capacity for finding ways to give birth easily and effectively.

The fetus ejection reflex

When a woman in heavy labour is confronted with a fear inducing situation, the labour may be so well established that it would be impossible to slow it down, and she may be so immobilised by the overwhelming nature of the contractions that "fight or fight" is physically impossible. Given these circumstances, often present during transition or the last moments of second stage, a sudden rush of adrenalin will have an opposite effect on the woman's body and instead of slowing or postponing the birth, it speeds labour up, to enable the baby to be born immediately. Instead of the adrenalin inhibiting oxytocin it causes a surge, followed by one or two huge contractions and the precipitate birth of the baby. The reason for this phenomena, first described by Niles Newton (Newton 1966), is to effect rescue of the mother and baby from a potentially dangerous situation. Instead of being immobilised by heavy labour, it can be advantageous to have the baby born as quickly as possible, so the mother is free to stand and fight or carry her baby away.

The stimulus for the rush of adrenalin may be obvious (many babies have been born very quickly once forceps are produced) or more psychological in nature. During transition, many women are frightened by the strength and power of the contractions and express this fear verbally — "I can't do this", "just get the baby out", "I can't take any more of this". Sometimes, even very negative comments may be heard — "Just give me a caesarean", "I want to die". Perhaps this is the "moment of truth" for many women, when they face the need to find the resources to survive the onslaught of a tumultuous transition. It may be very important to allow women to have the experience of conquering an overwhelming personal crisis, as a way of promoting confidence and self-esteem in the new mother. Encouraging expression of her negative thoughts (which she may not remember afterwards anyway) may be necessary to enable her to face the fear and deal with it. Reassurance or distraction may not, perhaps, be desirable or beneficial in the long run.

Sudden cooling of the body can also be interpreted as a threat to survival with a resultant surge in adrenalin leading to a fetus ejection reflex. Stepping out of a warm bath can trigger this reaction, and a wise midwife will keep a delivery pack nearby in the bathroom when women are using warm water for pain relief in labour.

Adrenalin and the baby

The baby also produces catecholamines (nor-adrenalin) in response to stresses of labour. During uterine contractions there is a reduced blood flow to the placenta, and to counteract any detrimental effects of this, the placenta stores oxygenated blood in between contractions, to ensure the baby's continued supply. An additional measure is provided by the production of nor-adrenalin by the baby. This has the effect of shunting the available blood to those parts of its body where it is most needed — the heart, the lungs, the brain. In this way the baby is able to function normally during labour.

In addition, it has been shown that the production of catecholamines (in particular, nor-adrenalin) by the baby during the labour better prepares it for healthy functioning after birth. The production of nor-adrenalin, amongst many other effects: mobilises the brown fat in the baby's body to produce heat and help maintain temperature after birth; dilates the pupils to encourage the mother to make eye contact; increases blood sugar levels to provide energy and is involved in the production of the surfactant that facilitates the absorption of the liquid in the baby's lungs following birth. Further descriptions of the usefulness of nor-adrenalin to the baby during birth are contained in a fascinating article published in New Scientist (Lagercrantz et al. 1986).

If the mother produces excessive catecholamines in response to anxiety, fear or stress, the baby can suffer from a lack of oxygen due to the reduced blood supply to the mother's internal organs, including the placenta. In turn the baby will react by producing excessive adrenalin, increasing the possibility of fetal distress and perhaps contributing to respiratory distress and metabolic acidosis. Therefore, it is vital that all sources of anxiety for a woman in labour be kept to a minimum, and that every attempt is made to enable the mother to labour with her own hormonal system intact, and with as little intervention in the birth process as possible.

References

Lagercrantz H. & Slotkin T. 1986, 'The "stress" of being born', *Scientific American*, April, pp. 92–105.

Newton N. 1971, 'Trebly sensuous woman', *Psychology Today*, no. 98, pp. 68–71.

—— 1978, 'The role of the oxytocin reflexes in three interpersonal reproductive acts: coitus, birth and breastfeeding', *Clinical Psychoneuroendocrinology in Reproduction*, Proceedings of the Serono Symposia, Academic Press, vol. 22, pp. 411–418, London.

Newton M. 1987, 'The fetus ejection reflex re-visited', *Birth*, vol. 14, no. 2.

Newton M., Foshee D., Newton M. 1966, 'Experimental inhibition of labour through environmental disturbance', *Obstet Gynecol*, vol. 67, pp. 371–377.

Russell, J. 1982, 'The rationale of primitive delivery positions', *Brit J of Obstets and Gynae*, vol. 89, pp. 712–715.

Chapter 6

HOW CAN I HELP?

Birth *can* be a most empowering experience for a woman. An enormous sense of satisfaction and achievement can result from weathering the power of birth, especially when she does it herself using her own innate resources. Part of the reward of birth is the self-discovery that comes from accessing innate instincts and acting on spontaneous needs. Observing this process of self revelation and growth in women is the special privilege of the midwife, for it is she, as an invited guest, who has the great honour of being present during this intimate time in a woman's life.

As we have seen, in the previous chapter, the process is governed by a delicate balance of hormones, designed to promote safety and encourage successful outcomes. This system will work well provided that it is able to flow unhindered.

The main purpose of self-help measures is to enhance the natural flow of oxytocin and endorphin and to reduce or eliminate adrenalin, bearing in mind that women react in different ways and a comfort measure welcomed by one, might become a source of annoyance for another. Once labour is well established the endorphins themselves will assist her to manage most of the labour without the need of additional help, and her supporters can then withdraw to maintain more of a protective, watching brief. It is in the early stages that self help measures can be particularly useful, to avoid adrenalin being produced early and stalling the onset of established labour. If it seems impossible for her to get her own natural painkillers working due to distress she may need to consider pharmacological pain relief, and this will be considered separately.

The last week/s of pregnancy

Towards the end of their pregnancy women focus in on themselves, and become more self-absorbed and sedentary. An acceptance of the inevitable often develops. Earlier, many women are still fearful of various things: possible problems with the labour, doubts about their ability to labour effectively, concerns about the well-being of the baby, potential complications, etc. Women spend much time thinking about these and other personal issues during the last weeks, (probably assisted by the rising level of endorphins during this time) and perhaps as a result of this inner reflection, learn that after all, it is too late to go back.

For some, however, the last weeks of pregnancy can mean the development of a complication, such as raised blood pressure, which adds extra stress to general uncertainty. Others just worry about the basic question "How will I know I am in labour?" to the extent that the resultant anxiety triggers adrenalin production sufficiently to block the low levels of oxytocin in their systems and the initiation of labour is delayed, perhaps to the point of going past their anticipated birth day. For these women, the scheduling of an induction often reduces the fear ("I know I will be in labour on Tuesday, so I don't have to worry about being unsure") and they go into spontaneous labour on their own, avoiding the induction.

Women with anxieties of any kind need caring attention and support that emphasises the positive. There are several useful self-help measures for the last weeks of pregnancy you could offer:

➡ Provide a listening ear — be an empathetic listener to any fears or anxieties she needs to talk about.

➡ Be quietly positive about her abilities, whilst not down playing the unknown quality of the event about to unfold. Saying "I am sure you will do well" can sound insincere since it is based on conjecture unless she has already given birth well. These kinds of comments may undermine her trust in you.

➡ See that she has good food, plenty of rest and avoids strenuous activity. Going into labour after a busy day with little rest means labouring with fewer reserves of energy. Assistance with child minding or housekeeping, perhaps arranged through community services or provided by her family are practical ways of enabling her to rest.

Going beyond her "due" date

Once the estimated date for the birth has passed, many women become frustrated and bored, and are therefore very vulnerable to suggestions of induction. As induction is one well-proven route to an eventual caesarean section, starting labour in this way cannot be recommended unless there is a clear case of medical need. If a woman and her baby can be shown to be perfectly healthy and in no danger, the problem then changes to one of supporting her while she waits. There are many things a midwife or support person can do:

→ Carefully reassess her due date. Many women rely on ultrasounds or calculations made by caregivers based on her last menstrual period. Many women have a good idea of when the baby was conceived, making a very useful starting point. Taking an individual history, including the length of menstrual cycles and family history will be necessary.

→ Check for signs that the pregnancy is coming to an end. The baby engaging in the pelvis, the ripening of the cervix and increased Braxton Hicks contractions can all be signs of approaching labour. Women can be shown how to check their own cervix: explain that an unripe cervix feels like her nose (pointy, sticking out, firm knob on the end) whereas a ripe cervix feels more like her parted lips (retracted, squashy and slightly open).

→ Encourage her to find some simple projects to keep her occupied. Many women arrange their diaries so that all social activity stops about the due date, in readiness for the expected birth. When labour doesn't begin according to the schedule, disappointment and anxiety can set in. Planning some simple events, such as going to a movie, having a haircut, seeing special friends or going out for dinner, can give her something to anticipate apart from the birth, and these kinds of activities can easily be cancelled if necessary.

→ Keep her thinking positively. Point out the special nature of this unexpected bonus of additional time, and the opportunity it offers for sheer self indulgence. This kind of personal time will not be available again for many years! Reminding her that waiting until the baby is ready reduces the risk of accidental prematurity from an untimely induction, and increases the chances of a straightforward labour and birth. This may help her focus on her primary goal of giving birth to a healthy baby.

→ Suggest some self-help ideas for stimulating labour: sex, accompanied by orgasm and locally applied prostaglandins (from the semen) can help ripen the cervix; nipple and clitoral stimulation will increase circulating oxytocin levels; warm baths and massage can lower adrenaline levels and reduce anxiety.

During first stage

Early labour

Pinpointing the start of labour is often impossible. Frequently the pregnancy slowly evolves into labour without clear cut events marking the borderline. Before labour settles into a regular pattern the best form of self-help is to get on with life, and continue with normal daily activities. This is not the time to begin charting contractions, timing intervals or consciously relaxing. Going about one's business, especially maintaining normal routines of eating and sleeping are very important. Some women become exhausted very quickly from "playing at labour", and feel demoralised when hours pass with little change. These early warning signs are nature's way of signalling that labour is coming so that last minute "nest building" can be completed. Once labour has established it will be impossible to focus on anything else, so this pre-labour phase can be useful in helping a woman to feel "ready" to give birth.

For some, symptoms of early labour might occur over several days. Research has shown that the Braxton-Hicks contractions gradually increase in severity during the night time hours over a period of 3–5 days, before an as yet unidentified "switch" turns the oxytocin level up instead of down as dawn approaches, resulting in true labour beginning (Nathanielsz 1994).

A woman can be said to be in true labour when there are firstly, contractions and secondly, the contractions show a consistent pattern, rhythm and increasing strength. The time between the contractions is irrelevant for assessing progress as there are many variations — a more reliable guide is the length and strength of the contractions themselves.

Self help in the first part of labour

At first, while the contractions are mild, you can encourage her to:

➡ Maintain normal daily activities. Support people may like to go to work as usual. Women in early labour often appreciate some time on their own, to get to know how their bodies are responding and to prepare emotionally and psychologically. They do not need to be watched or guarded!

➡ Avoid fatiguing exercise. This is not the time to go for a five mile walk to try and get labour established more quickly. Rest, even sleep, might be more useful in this regard — sleeping is a simple way of keeping adrenalin levels low.

➡ Eat and drink normally, and have a snack in the evening before going to bed if there are signs she might be labouring during the night.

➡ Recognise that this is the time when she can discover the answer to another nagging question: "What does labour feel like?" Many women worry about this, especially during the first pregnancy. These early contractions offer a "getting to know you" time, when individual responses to the contracting uterus can be noted, and some early experiments to increase comfort can be tried.

➡ Get organised: pack the car for the trip to hospital, walk the dog, finish basic household chores etc. so that when the time comes to make the move from home to hospital, there is order, not chaos.

➡ Phone support people and alert them to the situation. People need time to arrange their own affairs before they can make themselves available for an extended period to support a woman in labour. A second call can be made when their actual presence is needed, and when the woman has a clearer idea of who she would like to be with her at that time. (Some women will have invited several people to assist, and when the birth begins, discover they want only one or two of the selected team).

➡ Sort out child care for other siblings. Knowing that other children are settled and happy can relieve the woman of another potential source of worry in labour.

➡ If the membranes have broken, make sure she has plenty of protection to collect the inevitable dribbles of amniotic fluid that come with each contraction. The feeling of a trickle of fluid running down the leg is especially inhibiting and can be very embarrassing. She might feel most secure sitting on a toilet for extended periods.

➡ If the membranes have broken and there are no other signs of labour, avoid creating a potential source of worry. Many hospitals have strict protocols in place for this eventuality, usually involving an immediate visit to the hospital for assessment and the imposition of a time limit before intervention (induction) is begun. Once the health and well being of the woman and her baby have been checked through appropriate questioning (it can be done quite effectively over the phone), the woman can be presented with various options to consider: coming straight to hospital to be checked and then going home or staying in a pre-natal ward (not the labour ward as this will increase the likelihood of immediate intervention); checking into a nearby hotel or motel, if she has travelled a long distance; staying at home until labour begins; or staying at home for a given time and then going to the hospital. There are various possibilities according to the circumstances.

Recent research (Hannah et al. 1996) has shown that there is no greater risk of infection for the baby in being immediately induced over waiting for labour naturally and that rates of caesarean birth are the same in both groups. Hannah's study also showed that women don't like waiting for labour to start on its own, particularly if that wait extends several days — it may be that having waited 9 months, women are naturally eager to get the baby born, especially when there are signs that it is close.

If she does choose to stay in her own home, you can suggest she carries on as normal, eating well, sleeping as usual and taking showers (not baths). She can check the colour of the escaping amniotic fluid herself and note the baby's movements, in addition to taking her temperature regularly. She could also report to the midwife by phone if this is reassuring for her or for you.

This pre-labour phase can go on for some time, especially with the first baby. In general, women behave quite normally and can carry on with regular daily routines. After a while (hours or even days), companions will notice some important changes in her behaviour that herald the next phase of labour. The contractions become stronger and more rhythmical and are accompanied by responses indicative of endorphin production. It may take hours of irregular contractions before this time arrives and it can be recognised by the altered state of the woman:

- She wants to rest her legs (sinking towards to floor).
- Between the contractions she rests in the same position.
- She closes her eyes.
- Conversation stops, both during and between contractions.
- She shows signs of withdrawal.
- There is a need to concentrate, as the stronger contractions are accommodated.

Once these signs are present, it can be assumed that labour is truly established, as indicated by the evidence of endorphins within her system. If these kinds of behaviours are not appearing, especially when the contractions are seemingly strong and uncomfortable, then adrenalin may be mounting in response to external or internal influences. Remedial action might be needed (see page 107).

When you notice this shift in her behaviour, you need to alter your responses to match hers (staying in rapport). As she quietens down and withdraws, try talking less and in a quieter voice. Slow down your movements too, and spend more time sitting, even dozing yourself. Try to avoid asking her questions, and monitor her labour by noticing how she is reacting.

Two important aspects of physiology need to be kept in mind at all stages of labour, but particularly in these early stages.

1. Labour is faster and more efficient if the woman maintains an upright posture. The presenting part of the baby will press more effectively against the cervix and this stimulates oxytocin production, and therefore regular contractions. Lying down will reduce pressure on the cervix, resulting in a slow labour. In addition, when she is upright the weight of the contracting uterus and pressure of the baby is downwards against the pelvic floor muscles and outwards against the abdominal muscles. This is more comfortable than having the weight pressing against bone, nerves and other organs as will happen if she lies down.

2. The vertical position facilitates ease of movement, making it easier for her to adjust her position in response to contractions. Bending, swaying, rocking and turning are all easy to achieve when upright but almost impossible when recumbent. Pregnant women will already have discovered this from their attempts to find a comfortable way to sleep.

Once she enters the altered state of consciousness that characterises established labour it is important to maintain a safe and protected environment, so that the flow of endorphins and oxytocin will not be hampered. Ways of doing this are outlined below.

General strategies for increasing her comfort at home

Women find it easy to respond spontaneously to the needs and demands of their bodies in labour when they are in their own homes. They can do as they please, and there is never the need to seek permission of others, or to be concerned about what is acceptable in labour. Even so, some women, particularly those having their first babies, often "play" at being in labour too soon, and adopt behaviours they think are required or appropriate, perhaps influenced by what they have been told or read in books. If you notice this is happening, you can remind her to forget what she has learned, and use the inner messages from her body to guide her. You can also offer some general strategies:

➡ Keep up the drinks — about a cup every hour is a rough guide.

➡ Remind her to use the toilet every few hours to keep her bladder empty. The walk to the bathroom will help her stretch her legs.

➡ Warm socks and loose comfortable clothing will assist. Keeping her knickers on will help maintain her privacy — she may need to wear sanitary pads to collect leaking amniotic fluid.

➡ Soft music may be welcome in the background. Try to keep other noise to a minimum.

➡ Quieten down your own activities. Talk infrequently, avoid questioning her, and keep your voice low or at a whisper. Try to keep other people away, or else give them very low key tasks.

➡ Anticipate her needs, and assist her without fuss or too much distraction. If her mouth looks dry, offer sips of water or a sweet to suck. If she seems hot, wipe her brow or the back of her neck with a cold wet washcloth. If she seems shivery, wrap her up in a blanket.

➡ If, as her caregiver, you need to check her or the baby, do this very quietly, with a minimum of talk and disturbance. When women are labouring well, and their own natural hormones are flowing freely, it is very unlikely that the baby will be in any distress or that she will have a problem herself. Most of the complications that arise in labour stem from an intervention that has caused side effects.

➡ Support people need to eat and sleep to conserve their own energy and reserves. Encourage them to take meal breaks. If they are unwilling to leave, offer foods that have no strong odours — garlic flavoured crisps, strong salami and spicy cooked foods may not be appreciated! Try fruit, nuts, sandwiches and milk based drinks instead. If the labour is going to be prolonged (often there are early indications of this) a small team of helpers who are able to take turns can ease the strain on a single support person. Those not immediately involved can nap. Support people often find it very hard to leave a woman in labour, since it can seem like the breaking of a commitment and trust, and it can be easier for them to take necessary breaks if they can be sure that nothing will change in their absence, and that her needs will continue to be met in the same ways.

Positions

Encourage her to move around until she finds a suitable place to labour. Some women will choose their bedroom, others find a smaller area, like a bathroom, more contained and private. The garden has appeal for some women. As labour establishes and develops she will become more spaced out and dreamy, as though in a trance. She may begin to feel tired, and seek ways in which to rest.

This is a critical moment, as the usual reaction to the need for rest is to find somewhere to lie down, especially if a bed is available. You may need to remind her at this point that lying down will not only slow labour, but make it more difficult to get comfortable. She will remember the problems she has had in finding comfortable sleeping positions over the last weeks of her pregnancy, yet she can probably also remember times when she has been able to fall asleep watching television or as a passenger in a car. These experiences may help reinforce the idea that it is quite possible to sleep while sitting up, provided that there is sufficient support. When a woman in labour is acting instinctively rather than intellectually, a natural tendency is to lie down on a bed if she is feeling tired, since this is a learned response we reinforce each

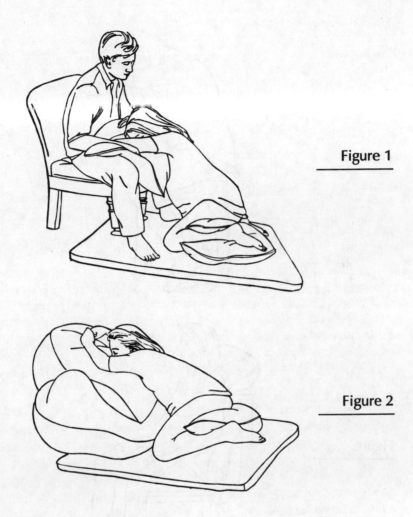

Figure 1
_____

Figure 2
_____

day. Encourage her to find ways of propping herself up against pillows etc. so that she is well supported. This can be achieved in several ways, shown in figures 1, 2, 3 and 4. If the back of the chair is too low, try using the ironing board (fully adjustable) to support the pillows (figure 5).

Once she is settled, and comfortable, she may stay in the same position for some time. It is not necessary for her to move unless she wants a change, or needs to relieve aching legs etc. Some women will want to walk about, swaying, rocking and generally using movement to encourage the baby to turn and descend.

65

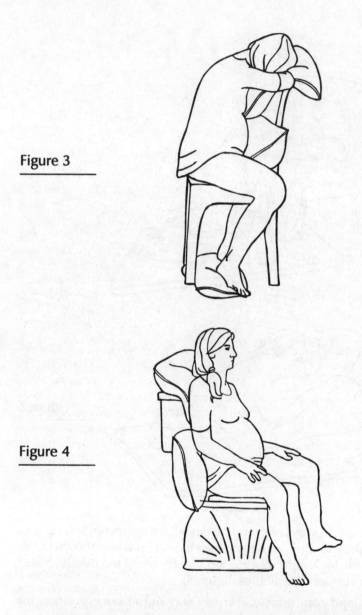

Figure 3
_____

Figure 4
_____

Try not to be prescriptive with your suggestions for comfortable positions. Instead of saying "why don't you try using this chair like this", you could say "some women find a chair positioned like this helps". Once her endorphins are flowing well, she will find it easier to respond to the inner messages from her body, and offering advice can interrupt this process of self discovery. A

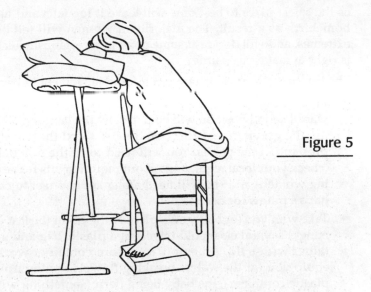

Figure 5

general comment such as "women seem to be able to find their own ways of getting comfortable given time" is a clear invitation to experiment.

This middle part of the first stage of labour can take some time. There may be a period of adjustment at the onset of established labour as she comes to terms with the new and stronger sensations that have developed. At first she may seem unsettled and restless as she experiments with various ways of getting comfortable, but as she discovers what works for her, she will once again find her own rhythm and coping mechanisms. As this happens, the support team can also relax, settling in with their roles and tasks and saving their own energies for the stronger labour to come.

Going to hospital

At some point in labour, women sense that the time is right to go to the hospital (unless they are planning a home birth). Many fathers, anxious and uncertain about being with a labouring woman and feeling the burden of responsibility, often want to take her there before she is ready. There can be no specific, identifiable indicator of the best time for this move. The time between the contractions is often given as a guide ("come in when the contractions are 5 minutes apart"), yet this may not reflect either the nature of her labour, or her response and reactions to it. It is best to rely on her own feelings about when she wants to go the hospital, and her interpretation of how the labour is progressing. Some women will want to go as soon as the first intermittent contractions start, as they are very fearful of staying at home and see hospital as the safest place to be. Some will leave it too late, and have an unplanned homebirth as a result. The majority of women will fall between these two extremes, and will decide at some point in an established labour that the time is right to make this journey.

The trip to the hospital is rarely comfortable. You could try:

➡ Positioning her on hands and knees in the back seat of the car. This forward leaning position will help to slow the labour a little, through reducing the gravitational effect on the baby and the resultant sensations of pressure in the pelvis. You will need to fit the seat belt as best you can (check your local regulations about requirements for seat belts for labouring women) and she will need a blanket or sheet to cover her, and perhaps a pillow for her head.

➡ Take with you (or better still, place in the car in the last weeks of the pregnancy) several clean, old towels in a plastic bag and a plastic food container with a lid. An empty ice-cream container works well. This will equip you for the waters breaking (towels to mop up), feeling sick (the plastic container), the baby being born (something with which to wrap the baby) and a container for the placenta, should it arrive too. Of course, none of these events may occur, especially if the trip is short, but if any distance needs to be covered, or there is a chance of traffic delays, then being prepared can be reassuring.

➡ An alternative position would be to sit her on the edge of the back seat, leaning over the front passenger seat, with its back pushed right forward. This tends to be less comfortable, as any bumps in the road will be more noticeable.

➡ Packing the car at the beginning of labour will save any last minute rush to get organised and avoid delays. When she says she wants to go to the hospital, she will want to go right away.

Settling in at the hospital

The manner in which a woman and her partner are greeted and admitted into the labour ward has a critical influence on the woman/partner/midwife relationship for the rest of her stay, as discussed previously in Chapter 4. Many subtle messages will be conveyed by the midwife — the ground rules about the conduct of the labour and the expectations of the woman as a patient. Admission procedures are usually presented as routines, indicating that there is a well-worn system for handling labours that the woman is expected to follow. Of course, women usually accept that hospitals need to have some systems, yet these must be balanced with the notion that birth is not an illness and that her labour is a unique personal experience. The potential for conflicts abounds: the offering of drugs and the use of technology when women have been exhorted during the preceding months to avoid anything that might impact on the health and well being of her baby; the often rigid application of unnecessary routine procedures, just because they have been listed in the hospital protocol; the limitations placed on her companions and the ways they can help her (limiting her food and drink, for example); even the language changes which may convey the impression, often through the use of "baby talk", that the woman is no longer a thinking adult but an inferior, incapable person who needs solicitous "care".

These influences must be recognised before strategies to minimise their impact can be devised. If the woman and her partner are regarded as visitors to your place of work, and ones with special privileges, it may enable you to make a warmer, more appropriate welcome rather than one that puts them in their place. Ideas for working with partners and other support people are described in Chapter 7. In addition:

➡ Discourage her from using the bed. There are some suggestions on how to do this described below.

➡ Turn down the lights to create a cosy, intimate atmosphere.

➡ Show the support people how to move the furniture in the labour ward, especially the bed.

➡ Get out the bean bags and floor mats and spread a sheet over them to increase their comfort.

➡ Show the support people where they can heat up hot packs, and fill a bucket with hot water for the hot towels (for how to use these, see below).

➡ Encourage the woman to stay in her street clothes while she is comfortable. She can change into something looser (not a hospital gown) when she is ready.

➡ Keep your initial observations to a minimum. Discourage her from sitting on the bed for these by seating her in a chair, with her partner in another chair close by. You too can sit down — this arrangement puts you all on an equal footing. Ways of doing the necessary observations are described below.

➡ If she has brought additional support people, apart from the father of the baby, make them feel welcome and useful, so that they don't turn the event into a social occasion. Take them aside and explain her basic needs for privacy, peace, quiet and non disturbance. Explain that the labour will be more productive, faster and more comfortable for her if they take a low profile, perhaps taking turns to be with her. Alternatively, allocate each person a specific task, such as supplying her with drinks, taking her to the toilet regularly, massaging her feet, or walking with her outside. People like to feel useful, and often feel ill at ease themselves in the unfa-

"Goody Bag" for Labour

For the labouring woman

* Her own clothes. A large soft cotton T-shirt works well.
* Dressing gown and slippers for privacy while walking around.
* Woolly socks, for cold feet in labour.
* Shower hat, for wearing in the bath or shower.
* Food and drink — less acidic drinks like apple juice are often preferred.
* Music of her choice and a portable cassette tape player
* Headphones so she has the full benefit of the music.
* Aromatherapy oils of her preference: for massage, using in the bath or with hot, wet towels.
* Washcloth for cold compresses.
* 4–5 handtowels, a pair of large rubber gloves and a bucket (for hot, wet towels).
* Spray bottle of fresh water, for her face.
* Sweets to suck on, or homemade juice ice blocks (put in the freezer in the labour ward kitchen).
* Mouth rinse (nice to get rid of the taste in her mouth if she has been sick).
* Flowers from her garden.
* The duvet from her bed.
* Her own pillows.

This is quite a list! The bucket can be used as a handy carry-all.

For the support people

* A spare pair of hands (support for the supporters), or someone on standby, if the labour is long.
* Food and drink. Choose foods without strong flavours or aromas. A Thermos of coffee or tea and small packs of fruit juice are useful.
* Loose, comfortable, washable clothing — you will be crawling around on the floor at times.
* Socks for your feet, so you can take off your shoes (noisy on some floors).
* Change of clothes, in case you get wet supporting her in the shower.
* Swimsuit or spare underpants, for getting in the shower or bath with her (you can be naked of course).

miliar environment of the hospital. Taking some time to familiarise them with the labour ward and her needs will minimise anxiety and discomfort — feelings the labouring woman is sure to sense if they are present in the room.

➡ Once you have settled her with her partner and belongings, give them some space and time to create their "nest". Encourage her to rearrange the room as she wishes and to find her own way of getting comfortable. Try saying "now we have completed the formalities, I am going to leave you to get settled. Feel free to make yourself at home and to create the kind of space you would like to welcome your baby. You can use the room any way you like, and I am sure you will find ways of using the chairs, bean bags, pillows and mats to make yourself comfortable and speed the labour. I will be back in a little while to see if there is anything else you need". It is important to make it clear that you know she can work out her own needs and find ways of settling herself into the rhythm of labour.

Many women become dependent at this time and will look to you for advice and inspiration. Avoid taking over and giving direct advice, as this will reinforce the idea that she is an inexperienced outsider, incapable of seeing to her own needs. Maintaining autonomy and independence is of utmost importance in building self-esteem and a sense of empowerment for pregnant and labouring women.

Making your observations

There are a number of baseline records you will need to make such as blood pressure, temperature, pulse, checking the position of the baby and its descent, and the fetal heartbeat. You will also check her urine for protein and ketones. At other times you will continue to check the progress of her labour, mainly focusing on the baby's position and reaction to labour. There is an art to making these observations non-invasively so that the woman and her labour remain undisturbed.

Before you begin, ask yourself: what observations are really necessary? The hospital may have partograms and protocols and insist that certain documentation is maintained. The need for general monitoring may be vital for safety, but there is little scientific evidence to support some measures such as routine electronic fetal monitoring. Once a labour *has* been disturbed through intervention, it becomes important to monitor the effect of these impositions on both the woman and her baby. Close attention to their well being will be essential and acute nursing care will be necessary. Apart from these issues, there is the potential for the tests themselves to cause problems, both physical (lying her down to check dilatation, for example, can reduce placental circulation) and psychologically (the Nocebo effect). Additionally, the general need for close surveillance needs to be re-evaluated, especially if the woman is labouring normally, with her own hormonal system intact. This woman needs the supervision of a midwife, using appropriate non-invasive techniques to judge progress and safety that are integral to midwifery.

Having decided on the observations to be made, you can then:

➡ Listen first. Women sound different in the various stages of labour, and this can often be a good indicator of progress by itself. The change from soft moaning to loud groaning may tell you that transition is underway and the insistent grunting of second stage is hard to miss!

➡ Observe her body language. Stand back and look at the way she responds to the contractions. This will often tell you what is happening. Women well settled into first stage are often quiet and withdrawn with their heads resting and eyes closed. They move little, and seem entirely in their own world. This continues for some time until the closer, more turbulent contractions of transition force her to move and shift position, setting up panicky feelings and generally distracting her with their strength and insistence. Feeling out of control is the characteristic emotion of this stage of labour and is a very good sign of progress. A break in the contractions following these behaviours often signals the resting phase before second stage. The sudden energy and action of giving birth, with its overwhelming urge to move, get upright and push are unmistakable.

All of these behaviours can be noted from a distance. Try sitting quietly in the corner for 10 minutes from time to time — you will be able to unobtrusively time contractions, note their strength and her responses. This is often more effective than either questioning or even hands on contact.

➡ Avoid asking questions. Having to think up answers requires brain power and cortical activity at a time when she needs to shut off her intellectual powers to stay in touch with her instincts. You can get most of the answers you need from accurate observation.

➡ Try not to stand in front of her. Placing yourself in a position facing her will encourage her to open her eyes to look at you. Once again, this will disturb her reverie and concentration. When you need to approach her, position yourself beside her, facing in the same direction as she is. She will know you are with her, yet be less likely to turn her head to make eye contact. You can observe her quite easily from the corner of your eyes. Getting down to her level, rather than standing over her will also be more effective in establishing rapport.

➡ Keep your voice low. Try whispering or speaking in a soft, low tone. Say as little as possible — this is not the time for cheery conversation. Encourage her partner to follow your example and discourage others who may be present from conducting side conversations within her hearing.

The main observation you will need to make is listening to the baby's heartbeat. If you use a sonicaid or pocket doppler this can be done with very little disturbance. You should not need to ask her to move very much as all you need is a small space to accommodate your hand and the doppler in a position for picking up the heartbeat. If she is not keen on the use of this equipment (some women like to limit their exposure to ultrasound) then you will need to use a Pinards or regular stethoscope. Quietly announce your intention to listen to the baby by placing your hand on her arm or shoulder to let her know you are with her and gently position the monitor. Simple feedback, such as a murmured "going well" or "just fine" is all that is generally needed.

Blood pressure, temperature and other basic checks can be done while she remains in whatever position she has chosen for comfort.

When you need to palpate, you can ask her to sit on the edge of a chair, place a firm pillow behind her and have her lean back. If you support her head with another pillow (or lean her head against her partner, standing behind) and raise her feet slightly, her abdominal muscles will be relaxed, and she will be almost horizontal, and easy to reach, even from a seated position. An alternative would be to position her on a bean bag on the floor. It may be awkward at first, but think about the psychological implications for the woman of doing it this way compared with the standard approach. Your confidence will build with practice.

Think twice about doing an internal examination. Her behaviour will often give valuable clues as to the progress of labour, and a vaginal examination should only be used when a manual assessment is essential, for example, before administering drugs, or to confirm a diagnosis suggested by other observations. Each internal examination increases the chance of infection, is uncomfortable for the woman, and is very disruptive of the labour process. For those women who have a history of previous sexual abuse it may be especially distressing, even to the point where their acute anxiety interferes with their progress in labour.

Internal examinations can be done with the woman off the bed and this is a basic skill that all midwives need to master. If she is sitting on a chair she will have to raise her bottom so that you can reach her, which will likely leave her standing. If she is kneeling down or sitting on her heels (perhaps leaning forward over a bean bag or chair) then she may also need to lift up a little. When women are in more upright positions, there are two basic options for carrying out the examination: you can either approach her from behind, or from the front.

If you ask her to lean forward, and position yourself behind her, you will have the problem of the baby seemingly being "upside down", that is, rotated through about 180 degrees. In addition, reaching the baby can be awkward, since the angle of the vagina will mean a long reach and the need to perhaps turn your hand over so the pads of your fingers are against the baby's head. For the woman who is unable to see what is going on because you are behind her, your actions could be interpreted as an "attack from the rear" and alarm her.

An easier way to manage the vaginal examination is to ask the woman to raise her shoulders so that she is vertical. Since she is likely to be leaning forward over pillows, a bean bag or her partner, this will not be difficult. The supports can be moved back a little to allow you easier access (figure 6).

The partner can stand behind so she has somewhere to lean. You will be kneeling in front of her (an appropriate position for the midwife) and you will be able to reach the baby easily. The increased gravity when she is vertical encourages the baby lower in her pelvis, making it closer to the exit and therefore easier to locate. The woman can see what you are doing and, being above you, she will find it easier to stay in charge, thus maintaining her autonomy. Remember that she will be looking at your face — think of what your expression might be indicating!

Figure 6

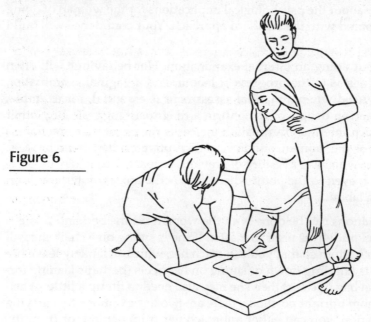

Once you have completed your examination, reposition the pillows, bean bag or chair so the woman can lean forward again and get comfortable. She will not have needed to move more than her trunk, and this will create the least disturbance for her.

General strategies for increasing her comfort in the hospital

Many of the strategies that were used while she was at home can also be used once she is in the hospital. The unfamiliar, often clinical atmosphere of the hospital poses special challenges for her support team whose role is to create as home-like a setting as possible in which she can labour safely. Paying attention to detail and viewing the hospital surroundings as though through her eyes will enable you to develop sensitivity to her needs and evaluate her responses to her surroundings. Some specific measures that may help include:

➡ Turn the lights down to create a cosy, intimate feeling. Low lighting automatically encourages everyone to whisper and tiptoe, which ensures peace and quiet. Dim lighting also reduces the visual impact of the equipment and the clinical atmosphere which is sometimes difficult to change in hospital labour wards. Dimmer switches are ideal, but if they are not fitted, try turning the lights off altogether, or rotating them so they are directing the beam against a wall. A small plug-in bedside lamp would be useful, and it can be placed on the floor or in a corner to reduce the light further. Heavy curtains that can be drawn in daylight hours are also useful.

➡ Make sure she is warm enough. The temperature in labour wards is often adjusted for staff comfort, and this could mean cool, dry air from central air conditioning. Keep her feet warm with thick woolly socks, and drape a blanket over her (figure 7) if necessary. Some women find that clothes become restrictive as labour progresses, yet if she is cold her body will react by producing adrenaline, which will slow progress. A sheet or blanket around her will keep her warm and will not feel as tight and uncomfortable as clothing.

➡ Maintain her fluids with regular drinks. Juices offer additional nourishment, and the less acidic juices such as apple or berry are often better tolerated than orange juice. Fruit flavoured ice blocks are also a useful alternative if she doesn't want to drink volumes of liquid.

➡ Encourage her to keep her bladder empty by offering her a bedpan or taking her to the toilet every 2–3 hours.

Figure 7

Positioning

Encourage her to find a comfortable position (away from the bed, of course!). Once she has settled, take a general look at her and check if there is some way you could add to her comfort. Some useful questions to ask yourself (don't expect her to respond to these, these are for your private use):

- Is her head resting on something? This will help her keep her eyes closed, conserve her energy, and tip her body forward taking pressure off her lower back. This forward tilt is the natural position for the uterus as it contracts.

- Is she fairly vertical? Being upright will keep the contractions coming steadily and productively.

- How are her feet and legs? Any constrictions may lead to cramping and numbness, which will add to her discomfort and force her to change position.

- If she fell asleep like this, would she fall off or fall over? She needs to be well supported so she can doze and completely let go.

If you feel that some modifications need to be made to increase her comfort, make these as quietly and unobtrusively as possible. Try to build on what she has devised for herself and avoid creating the impression that you know bet-

---

Ideas for keeping women off the bed during labour and birth

Pre-natal check ups

- Can these be done without the woman reclining on a bed?
- Before she arrives into the labour ward:
- Arrange the room
- move the bed to one side or set it up as a chair (if you have modern hydraulic birthing beds),
- position 3 chairs (stacking chairs need little storage space) in the middle of the room, one for her, another for her partner and one for you,
- place a cover on the bed for protection when you put her belongings on it.

During labour and birth

- Encourage her to get comfortable away from the bed ("labour is faster, more comfortable and easier to manage if you move around and stay vertical").
- Provide a mat for the floor and a sheet to cover it. Use the mattress off the bed if you have no other suitable mat available.
- Offer bean bags and extra pillows.
- A variety of chairs, preferably with straight backs and no arms encourages experimentation.
- Birth stools are comfortable for many women in early second stage.
- Learn to do your observations with the woman in any position.
- Protect her right to stay in her chosen position — avoid moving her for someone else's convenience.
- Have a low stool for your own use, to protect your back from excessive bending.
- A portable lamp to provide illumination for stitching might be useful if she is off the bed following the birth of the placenta.

---

ter about what is good for her than she does herself. The following ideas are drawn from observations of many labours and can be offered to her as gifts from other women who have found them helpful during birth.

If she is on the floor, she will need a firm mattress or pillow under her legs. A rolled up towel or pillow (strong rubber bands will stop them from unrolling) under her ankles will prevent strain on her feet (figure 8). Alternatively, if she is on a thick mattress, place the edge of it under her ankles, so her feet hang over the edge.

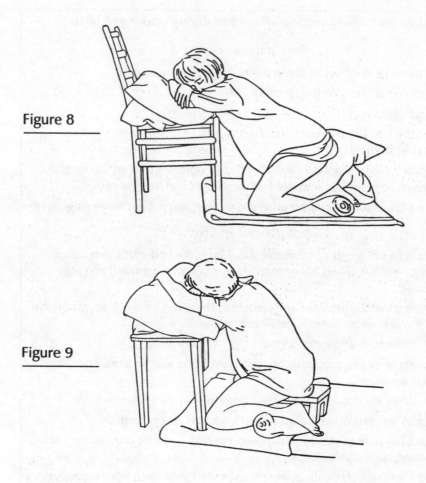

Figure 8

Figure 9

Pillows behind the knees will raise her buttocks and decrease congestion in her legs. If she has heavy thighs and calves you may need to lift her up higher, perhaps through offering her a padded footstool to sit on (figure 9). This will also reduce pressure on her knee joints and provide solid support.

Chairs can be used in a number of ways. Hospitals are often equipped with lounge or rocking chairs and you will need to find a chair without arms, and possibly two, to try these positions. Simple stacking chairs are ideal and a small pillow placed on the seat will soften hard plastic seats and counteract any lip around the edge of the seat itself. Place a pillow underneath her tummy (figure 10), so that she is well supported and has no back strain. This will also provide a way of positioning a hot pack against her lower tummy to soothe localised pain in that area.

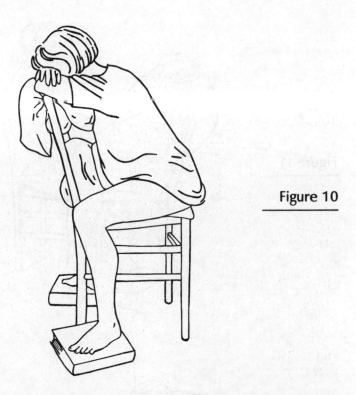

Figure 10

Try to get her back as straight as possible. If she is slumped forward, the uterus will be tucked hard against her diaphragm, and this can lead to the development of a "stitch" or general discomfort. A straight back can be achieved in two ways: either by raising her head and shoulders with a higher support in front, or by sliding her buttocks back onto an extended support behind.

Two chairs placed with their seats touching facilitates this second manoeuvre (figure 11), with the added bonus of a place for the partner to sit. The hospital bed table can be used in much the same say as the ironing board was used at home, provided the wheels are chocked to stop it moving away.

Try and position her chair, bean bag or mat away from the centre of the room, facing the wall or a corner. Making her the centre of attention will encourage interaction from others, so try and tuck her away in a corner or behind the bed or door. With her back to the door she is less likely to look up each time someone enters the room.

Many women enjoy the automatic privacy that the toilet offers. Staying in the bathroom can also be a way of escaping from the noise and bustle of busy

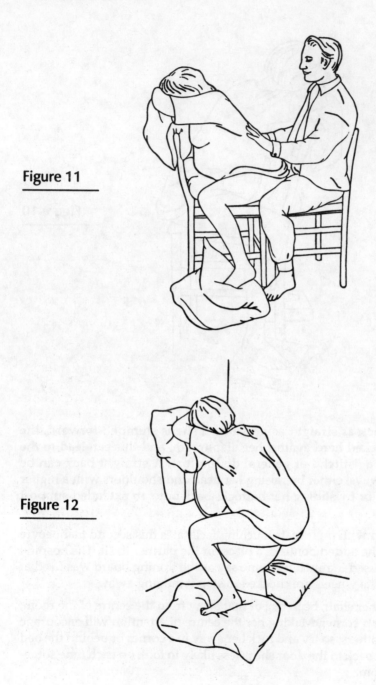

Figure 11

Figure 12

Figure 13

times in labour wards, such as the hand-over at the end of shifts or the flurry of activity in the early morning as the doctors do their rounds and the hospital stirs for the day. An additional benefit is that adults automatically respect the right of those in the bathroom or toilet to privacy and it is unlikely that she will be disturbed. You will need to make her comfortable on the toilet: pillows or rolled towels under her feet to take pressure away from her thighs (the toilet seat is usually higher from the floor than most chairs); sitting her back-to-front so she can rest her head forward on the cistern (a rolled towel placed doughnut-style around the button and under a pillow will avoid continuous flushing as she leans against it) (figure 12); a sheet or blanket over her head to keep bright lights out of her eyes (if it is impossible to dim the lights in some other way) (figure 13).

Once she is comfortable, she may want to stay there for some time. There is no need to hurry her, and her labour will speed up once this kind of privacy and protection from interruptions is in place.

Other ways to relieve pain

Hot packs are welcome in labour to ease localised pain. Many women will have used a hot water bottle to soothe period pain and will know of the benefits to be gained from localised heat. Hot packs come in various forms and sizes: plastic bags in various shapes filled with a blue jelly that can be heated in a saucepan of hot water; wheat filled packs (even an old sock filled with wheat works well), again in various sizes, that are heated in a microwave oven; hydrocolator packs (canvas bags filled with clay that are heated in a water trough) often used by physiotherapists. Hot water bottles can also be used, but their rigidity and weight make them unsuitable in some situations. Hot packs can be positioned in various ways, and held in place by the careful placement of support pillows. Try one under her tummy held in place by a pillow. She might like to try sitting on one: a 500 ml IV pack makes a good hot pack (use a pack beyond its use-by date) as it is strong, a useful sausage shape, can be heated in the warming cupboard (not the microwave), and has enough flexibility to allow gentle bouncy movements. Women sitting on one of these can give themselves a welcome massage, to ease discomfort from deep vulval pressure.

Music can offer pleasant diversion, especially if it has been chosen by her. Using headphones will ensure that she receives the full benefit and this is a practical solution for blocking out other noises that might otherwise disturb or frighten her such as a woman having an noisy transition in the next room.

Massage and back rubs are often welcomed by women as ways of easing specific aches and pains. The person providing this service needs to take care of themselves, since massaging for hours can lead to back problems. Here are some hints for reducing the strain on the assistants:

➡ Position yourself behind the woman, to reduce twisting of your own back. This will be easier to achieve if she is not on a bed, but positioned as shown on a floor mat. She may need extra pillows or padding under her knees, in addition to the mattress or mat. Alternatively, she can sit back to front on a chair, with pillows for supporting her head and tummy.

➡ Get down to a comfortable working height (usually kneeling) to avoid bending (figure 14). Putting one leg up as shown, and changing as necessary, will enable you to move forward and back to reach her whole back, without excessive bending. This will protect your own lower back from strain.

➡ Massage strokes should be slow and rhythmical, using the whole hand with soft fingers. Applying localised finger pressure will quickly tire your own hands. Massage oil, containing a suitable aromatherapy essence such as lavender, will make massaging easier, and offer the added benefit of reducing the "hospital smell" in the room. For further information on the use of aromatherapy in labour there are useful references for exploring this form of pain relief in more detail (Tiran 1996; Fawcett 1993; Wesson 1995; Tiran & Mack 1995).

➡ Long strokes over her whole back can promote relaxation in between the contractions. Extending the stroke over her buttocks and down her legs

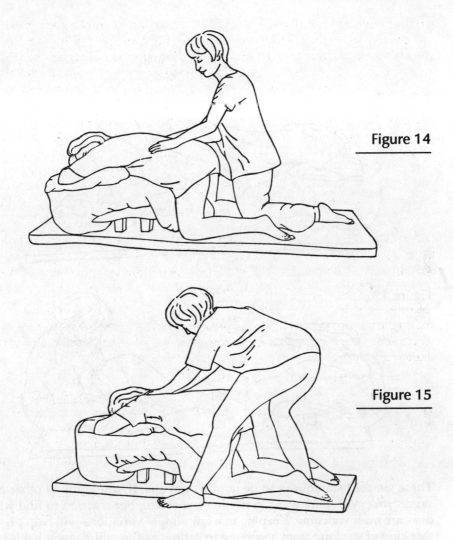

Figure 14

Figure 15

can relieve any muscular aches in those areas. The partner shown in figure 15 is standing, useful if the woman is tall, so her back can be reached
easily. Both knees are bent to reduce back strain and enable free movement back and forward during the massage stroke.

➡ Holding her over the shoulders and around her hips provides reassurance and reminders to let any tension go (figure 16).

➡ Simple foot massage, or just steady holding if she is ticklish, can be com-
forting. Women often find their feet becoming cold and holding in this
way can relax as well as warm (figure 17).

Figure 16

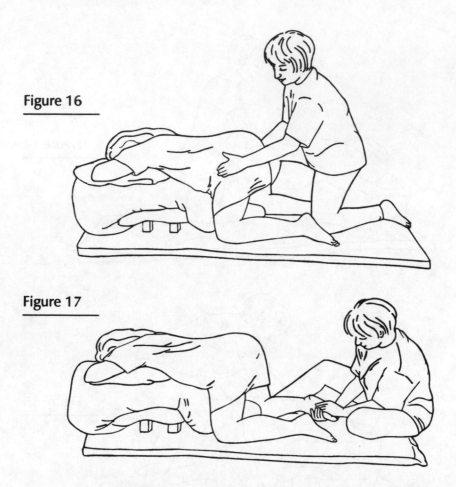

Figure 17

These simple techniques can be used by anyone. If you know of other massage strokes you may want to try them, checking her reaction to find which ones are most welcome. Keeping to a few simple variations will help prevent this kind of stroking from becoming irritating, as she will know what is coming next and will not have to stay alert for the next kind of touch. Your aim is to provide this kind of comfort without disturbing her trance-like state.

If the baby is in a posterior position

The best position for encouraging the baby to turn to an anterior position is to have the woman leaning forward, fully supported by pillows or a bean bag, with her back parallel to the floor. Her hips should be above her knees to allow her legs and trunk muscles to fully relax. Some additional measures can be added if the woman is experiencing chronic backache during labour:

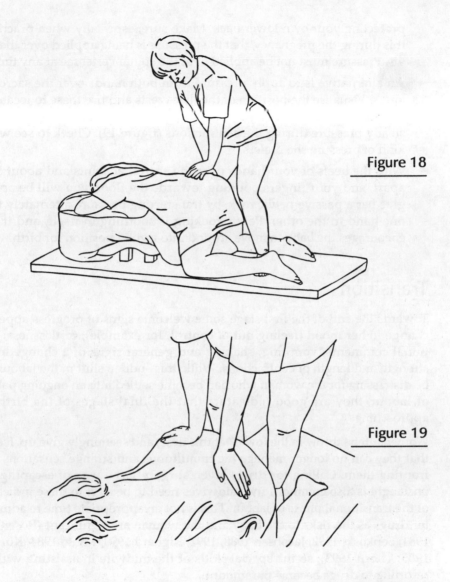

Figure 18

Figure 19

➡ Localised sacral pressure helps to counteract the pain of the baby's head against the sacrum. Position yourself in close (usually standing up, unless you are tall and can reach while kneeling). Place the heel of one hand over the heel of the other, on top of the sore area and, with your elbows locked straight, bend your knees to transfer some of your body weight to her pelvic area. Hold steadily for the duration of the contraction (figure 18). This action will make it easier to apply pressure whilst protecting your own lower back. Make sure, especially when practising this during the pregnancy, that the pressure is being applied over the pelvis. Pressure must not be applied over the spinal vertebrae at any time.

➡ An alternative is to apply pressure from both hands over the sacroiliac joints. Visualise the position of the iliac crests and use these to locate the sacrum at the back. Place your hands over the sacroiliac joints, and apply steady pressure during the contractions (figure 19). Check to see which kind of pressure she prefers.

➡ With the heels of your hands over the sacroiliac joints and about 5 cm apart, and your fingers pointing towards the floor, you will be able to give her a passive pelvic rock, by transferring pressure alternately from one hand to the other. Pelvic rocking is soothing in itself, and it also encourages the baby to move around into a good position for birth.

Transition

Towards the end of the first stage some welcome signs of progress appear: a change in her mood (feeling out of control, for example); restlessness; irrational comments; vomiting; shaking and general signs of a change in the strength and length of contractions. While this sudden shift in the labour can be distressing for the woman who had become settled into an ongoing pattern of labour, they are good indicators that the final stages of the birth are approaching.

Women often "throw in the towel" at this time, and seemingly give up, feeling that they can no longer manage the tumultuous and strange sensations confronting them. Calling for drugs (even surgery!) as a way of escaping this onslaught is also common, and midwives need to be alert to these indicators of the transitional phase of labour. This is not an appropriate time to administer drugs as the risks to the baby and the woman are significant (Rosenblatt 1981; Sepkoski 1992; Jacobsen 1988, 1991; Righard 1990; Kanto 1984; Kuhnert 1985; Thorp 1993), so the special skills of the midwife in assisting without resorting to drugs become paramount.

The first step is to establish that what you are observing is indeed indicative of the transitional phase of labour. This may be one occasion when an internal examination is useful, to check that the cervix is 7 or more centimetres dilated in a primiparous woman or at least 3–4 centimetres in a multiparous woman. A vaginal examination should always be undertaken before drugs are administered, and frequently it will be discovered that the cause of her distress is the normal turbulence of transition. If she is not well dilated, then her reactions may be a sign of panic and the appropriate action will be the standard measures for calming someone who is panicking (see page 32).

Helping women through this part of the labour requires skill, patience, acceptance and above all calmness and understanding from the midwife. Some specific measures you could try:

➡ Offer her privacy and personal space. Many women want to shout, move around, let off steam and generally let go at this point in the labour. She may feel more spontaneous and uninhibited if she knows she is by herself, with no-one watching or trying to intervene.

➡ Take care of the father and other support people. They will need reassurance that these are normal reactions and positive signs of progress. Keeping them occupied while she passes through this part of labour will reduce the effects of their anxiety on her responses.

➡ A change of scene might help. Moving her, perhaps to a smaller, more private room, such as the bathroom or toilet, will help to buy time and relieve her need for action of some kind.

➡ Telling her that this is the transitional phase of labour may encourage her. It won't reduce the intense pain and discomfort, but it may help her to know that it will be short lived. This is especially important is she is demanding drugs, since if she knows that second stage is imminent, many women will be able to manage a little longer if they know the baby will be born soon.

➡ Enable her to voice her feelings. This is not the moment to ask her to be quiet for the sake of others in neighbouring rooms. She must sense that you understand her protests and accept her need to shout out as normal. Giving voice to negative feelings may speed up labour, by triggering the fetus ejection reflex, described in Chapter 5.

Using water and heat

At this point in labour, labouring women and their midwives are looking for ways of easing the discomfort and pain, without using drugs. Water and heat, in various forms, can be especially useful, offering relief from the pain with no effects on the baby. As a new form of comfort, especially if not tried earlier in the labour, they have particular appeal, since the psychological benefit of having something extra available is quite powerful at this time. Another benefit of using a combination of water and heat is that setting it up will take some time, and often require her to move around (to get into a bath or shower, for example) and provide a change of environment — one which offers automatic privacy. Water and heat have other uses in labour, described below.

When to consider using warm water in labour and birth:

- When privacy is needed.
- During transition.
- If labour is stalled with no further dilatation.
- For removing a persistent anterior lip of cervix (bath).
- For calming a woman in a panic.
- To reduce a premature urge to push (bath).
- When her blood pressure is rising in labour (bath).
- To reduce pain (instead of drugs).
- To speed up labour (instead of a drip).

If you can offer her a bath or pool, try to have it ready about the time transition is anticipated. Take care with the water temperature (it should be no hotter than 37 degrees Celsius to avoid raising both her core temperature and that of the baby) and provide waterproof pillows for resting her head. Some padding might also be useful under her knees, especially if she is kneeling and leaning forward.

The shower is a good alternative, having the advantage of maintaining the full effects of gravity, which can speed the labour. She may choose to stand, kneel or sit, and will need appropriate support from plastic chairs or stools and padding (towels work well) under her knees. Her partner can join her in the shower, and this intimacy is often very welcome during transition.

If a shower, bath or pool is not available, then useful substitutes can be hot, wet towels. These provide the same kind of soothing comfort as other forms of water and heat, with some notable differences. The main disadvantages are that they cool quickly, and that they are very popular with women, so that once you start applying them, you will not be allowed to stop. Therefore, don't begin using them too soon in labour! Figure 20 shows how they are used:

➡ You will need a bucket, three or four hand towels (cloth nappies work very well) and a pair of rubber gloves to fit you or the support person. The parents can supply this equipment as part of their "goody bag".

➡ Fill the bucket with very hot water (perhaps topping it up from the tea kettle). The water will cool quickly once you start returning cold wet towels to the bucket.

➡ Place the bucket beside the woman. This will avoid running back and forth to a washbasin and the possibility of dripping water onto the floor (a safety hazard on vinyl flooring).

Figure 20

➡ Sit beside the woman, and wait until she gives a signal that a contraction is starting. Pull out a towel, speedily wring it out as hard as possible so that there is no water dripping, unfold and drape over the part of her body to be warmed. Women often like them applied to their lower backs, and also bunched under their tummies. Once you have the knack, it will take you about 20 seconds to wring out the towel, so you will be applying it at about the same time as she reaches the peak of the contraction. Leave the towel in place until the start of the next contraction.

➡ With the next contraction, take off the cold towel and replace with a hot one. You will find a rhythm developing. If there are two support people, it will be possible to use two towels at a time, perhaps one on her back and another under her tummy.

These magical aids for labour pain have been used by midwives for centuries (another great use for boiling water in labour) and have been part of the midwife's armoury of non-pharmacological pain relievers in the United States and Australia for over 15 years.

Summary

Bath/Pool

Advantages:

• Promotes privacy.

- Reduces risk of intervention.
- Reduces adrenalin automatically which in turn, promotes endorphin and oxytocin production.
- Encourages easy movement.
- Decreases the effect of gravity
- Reduces muscle tone: possible aid to dilatation, and reduction of stress on pelvic floor.
- Decreases pressure on aorta and inferior vena cava.
- Reduces load on the heart — reduces fatigue.
- Sensory stimulation (touch, warmth, proprioception) may "gate out" pain in the spinal cord.
- Reduces risk of dehydration if the water is at body temperature, as water is absorbed through the skin.
- The woman can stay in the bath for the birth if she wishes.
- Promotes midwifery skills.

Disadvantages:

- May not be available for all women.
- Decreases the effect of gravity.
- Can raise woman's core body temperature and this is turn can pose a risk to the baby of a raised temperature resulting in an increased need for oxygen.
- If problems develop with the baby, the woman will need to get out of the water.
- May increase perineal tears if submerged for long periods prior to the birth.
- Perineal tissues may become waterlogged, requiring a waiting period before stitching can take place.
- Theoretical risk of a water embolism if the placenta is delivered in the water.
- Water hard to keep clean.
- Wet floors and slippery surfaces could pose risks to caregivers.
- May cause back pain in caregivers due to increased bending.
- Requires plentiful supplies of hot water.
- Moveable pools need strong floors to support them when full.

Shower

Advantages:

- Promotes privacy.

- Reduces risk of intervention.
- Reduces adrenalin indirectly, lowering stress, and this in turn, promotes endorphin and oxytocin production.
- Gravity is not affected.
- Promotes ease of movement, as woman is upright.
- Water can be much hotter, as the woman is not immersed.
- Little risk of raising core body temperature, as she is not immersed.
- Heat can be localised.
- Woman can stay in the shower for the birth — just turn water off.
- Partner can accompany the woman to provide physical support.
- Partner may benefit from the shower as well.
- Promotes midwifery skills.

Disadvantages:

- May not be available for all women.
- Need a steady supply of hot water.
- Needs good ventilation to avoid overheating in steamy conditions.
- Woman can become dehydrated unless she drinks fluids regularly.
- Wet floors and slippery surfaces could pose risks.

Hot, wet towels

Advantages:

- Useful alternative if the bathroom is not available.
- Provides localised heat source.
- Not heavy, stay in place without support or holding.
- Effective form of pain relief.
- Can be used in conjunction with the shower, drip lines and TENS machines.

Disadvantages:

- Get cold quickly.
- Water in the bucket cools quickly and must be replaced every 20–30 minutes.
- Very intensive work for the support people.
- Very popular with women — she will not let you stop supplying them!
- Blisters on hands from wringing out towels for hours.
- Slippery wet floors unless the bucket is placed beside the woman.

General precautions

- Make sure the temperature of the water in the bath is no hotter than 37 degrees celsius.
- If there is prolonged rupture of membranes, immersion in a bath may increase risk of infection.
- Keep her well hydrated with regular drinks.
- Check the fetal heart regularly (using a waterproof sonicaid).
- Assess her before she enters the bath or shower to determine progress.
- Allow at least an hour for the benefits of water to have an impact on her labour.
- Avoid pulling the plug in a bath if the baby is being born — the baby may inhale water if it is only partially submerged.
- Have a delivery pack of basic equipment in the bathroom in case the baby is born quickly.

Second Stage

This could be described as the best part of labour: the baby is about to arrive, the anticipation is building, relief from the contractions is almost there and the rewards for all the effort are about to be discovered. There are mixed emotions too, of excitement, apprehension, exhaustion, elation, anxiety and amazement. This part of birth is to be savoured and enjoyed, forming as it does a brief bridge between the pregnancy and motherhood, a few moments suspended in time before the imagined baby becomes full blown reality. Women have only a few minutes to experience these emotions and revelations and they should not be hurried unless it is clearly necessary for the safety of the baby. She needs to give herself time to physically embrace her body's needs as well — the rest period before the pushing starts in earnest, a chance for the vagina and pelvic floor muscles to spread apart, an opportunity for the perineum to gently stretch around the baby's emerging head. Those present need only watch and wait, there is very little that needs to be done for her, as she can take charge and manage the birth herself, provided her innate abilities are recognised and encouraged.

This is especially important for caregivers, who often become increasingly concerned as the baby moves lower and it becomes more difficult to listen to its heartbeat. The option of a caesarean recedes as the baby advances, and it becomes a matter of waiting, sometimes with hope, for the safe arrival of the baby. This is where a strong belief in the innate safety of birth and that nature will once again make every effort to bring the baby safely into the world is essential. Having come so far (the nine months of the baby's growth and development and the hours of labour so far) it is unlikely for the short journey down the birth canal to be especially hazardous. Therefore, trust and faith, coupled with a good knowledge of the normal physiology are useful tools for the midwife at this point.

The conditions that have been established earlier to maximise efficiency and safety in labour should be maintained. Women may show different behaviours during birth, but they still need a supportive, non-invasive, private setting for their hormones to work well. Unfortunately, it is at this time, especially in hospitals, that the scene changes alarmingly: it is almost as if the woman, with her first constructive push, sends up a signal for action all round. In teaching hospitals and larger institutions the situation is made worse by the larger staff numbers. Students, additional midwives, the doctor and perhaps a paediatrician may materialise, adding to the general clamour and providing visual and audible distractions. The woman finds herself on a stage in the centre of the room, half naked and surrounded by strangers, with a spotlight shattering her privacy. Instructions are issued by the team and a chorus of exhortations can erupt from the side lines. No wonder many women find it hard to concentrate and push effectively in these circumstances. If, in addition, she also has an overwhelming urge to empty her bowels, the panicky feelings this causes (could anyone use a toilet successfully in these circumstances?) can slow progress, as she fights to ward off the unwelcome sensations.

It is imperative not to hurry the birth. Particular concerns centre around the important issues of preventing maternal and fetal distress and protecting the perineum. Suggestions for avoiding these situations are described below.

Women often become confused and unsure of what to do at this point in labour. They often assume passive, subservient positions, sometimes at the caregiver's request. Any animal lying on its back with its legs in the air is meekly submitting itself to domination, and this is no position for a woman needing to take charge and provide safety for her baby. Any woman who is requesting instructions about pushing or looking to caregivers for advice is risking losing one of the most significant moments in her life for self-discovery and personal growth. In a physiological sense, she may not even be in second stage, since the urge to push is usually so overwhelming and insistent that it invokes involuntary action on her part to work with her body. It may, however, be the conditions in which she finds herself that are affecting her natural instincts at this point, and this is where vigilance and support from the midwife can make a huge difference to the outcome, not only in terms of protecting the woman from unnecessary intervention, but in improving the safety of birth for the baby.

93

Avoiding fetal distress

Fetal distress is a very worrying event in labour, signalling, as it does, that the baby is suffering and in need to assistance. Prolonged fetal distress is not very common in normal, physiological labour, although periodic disturbances in the fetal heartrate can be detected in many labours, as the baby adjusts to the physical effects of the birth process. Once there has been intervention the baby needs to be watched carefully for any effects on its well being.

Keeping labour as normal as possible will produce the fewest risks to the baby. Measures to enhance natural physiology are discussed elsewhere. The following suggestions relate the second stage of labour, a time when it is sometimes difficult to monitor the baby, and the practicalities of rescue via a caesarean section are more difficult as the birth progresses.

- Encourage her to stay upright. This will open up her pelvis, speed the second stage and reduce the risk of compression of the inferior vena cava that could result in reduced blood flow to the placenta.

- An upright stance will also reduce the risk of the baby lying on its cord, causing compression.

- Encourage her to push only as she needs to, and to not hold her breath more than she has to. Breath holding is a natural response to the need to bear down, and women should be left to manage this as they wish. Enforced breath holding ("cheer squad pushing") is dangerous: sufficient pressure can build up within the chest cavity to reduce venous return to the heart and therefore cardiac output; the lack of breathing means that oxygen interchange is not occurring in the lungs; and the combination of these mechanisms can lead to fetal distress. Roberto Caldeyro-Barcia in the late 1970s clearly demonstrated how this form of management causes the distress it was designed to prevent, yet it still persists (Caldeyro-Barcia 1979).

- If there is a pause between first and second stages, with few contractions, or even none at all, enable her to rest. This period may last minutes or even hours, and provided the mother and baby show no signs of distress, it is advisable to wait. This recovery time will avoid incipient distress in transition becoming a chronic problem.

- If there are indications of distress, and the speedy birth of the baby is necessary, it may be faster and safer to position the mother in a deep squat and ask her to push forcefully. A woman worried about the health of her baby will produce mighty efforts if required, and this approach might save time over the more traditional method of employing forceps. It may not be essential to do an episiotomy in this circumstance either — the skin will tear naturally if necessary.

Avoiding maternal exhaustion

Many women become exhausted in labour because they have been made to work too hard. Hospital policies can also contribute to maternal exhaustion and the increased need for intervention. These problems can be reduced by:

- Offering her food in labour, particularly as labour starts.

- Offering her regular drinks. About a cup of liquid per hour is a rough guide to her needs. Choose non-acidic juices, cordials or just plain water. Flat lemonade is useful for nausea.

- Support her need for a rest following transition. Many women find their labours slow dramatically, or even stop completely for a period. This allows the mother and baby to regain their equilibrium and gather their strength for the birth to come. A resting phase for the baby is especially important if transient dips in the fetal heart were observed during the transitional phase of labour.

- When she needs to push, enable gravity to assist her by encouraging her to be vertical. This will open up her pelvis, speed the labour and reduce the effort she needs to make.

- Avoid telling her when to push. She will respond to the pushing urge quite spontaneously, and any instruction she is given is likely to lead to unnecessary pushing, which is exhausting. Remember that the uterus can birth the baby entirely on its own, and given gravity to assist the descent of the baby, the mother may not need to exert a lot of additional effort. Let her judge this for herself.

- Allow enough time for the second stage. There is no evidence that arbitrary time limits are of benefit, and a side effect of enthusiastic exhortations to push the baby out quickly may lead to exhaustion for the mother and perineal trauma.

General strategies for improving her comfort

Of course, this is where the woman giving birth in her own home has a huge advantage: she will not be disturbed by the arrival of strangers; no additional equipment will be wheeled in; no students will gather to witness the birth. Creating a similar kind of peaceful, private environment within the hospital poses a particular challenge for the midwife and it is at this very special time that a midwife needs to be particularly sensitive. The first step is to try and limit physical changes within the room:

➡ Avoid turning on the lights — they can be used later, if suturing is needed. The baby is more likely to open its eyes if the room is darkened, and the woman will feel less "on view" if the lights are dimmed.

➡ Keep all unnecessary personnel away. If students are to be involved (make sure you have the woman's permission well in advance), talk to them outside the room and explain that they need to remain quiet and stay in the background.

➡ Avoid moving her from her chosen position. If she has been encouraged to stay off the bed and has found a way to make herself comfortable using pillows, bean bags or the support of her partner, make it clear she does not need to move.

➡ Decide what equipment is essential, and place it near the mother. A sterile sheet under her on which to place the baby will be needed. Drapes, sterile washes or other invasive procedures can be abandoned. Essential equipment (very little, it will be discovered) can be assembled within reach.

➡ Avoid talking to her, especially to give her instructions about pushing. Safety is increased if the woman is left entirely to judge her own needs in second stage, particularly the amount of effort and the timing of pushes she needs to gradually bring her baby out. If she is listening to others telling her what to do, she may lose concentration and may push inappropriately (for too long, or too hard).

➡ If she is unsure about how or when to push, offering her a bedpan or suggesting she sit on the toilet for a while (if she is primip) can awaken her natural instincts. Sitting upright is a familiar position for elimination, and pregnant women have had plenty of practice! Nurses know that asking a bed-ridden patient to move their bowels whilst lying down is asking for an impossible feat, and that to achieve success they must prop the patient in a vertical position. In the same way, sitting women on a toilet or bedpan will encourage the baby to move lower and thus trigger the natural pushing urges created by pressure on the nerves around the vagina and anus and in the pelvic floor muscles.

If she has no urge to push, then reassessment is needed.

Is she is in true second stage? She may be fully dilated, yet still in the latent phase before the pushing contractions develop.

Her baby may still be slightly transverse and unable to move down until it turns a little more. Walking around and pelvic rocking may help move the baby into a better position.

If she has been given an epidural it may not have worn off enough to enable the stimulation of the nerve endings in the vagina and pelvic floor musculature to trigger the release of oxytocin.

Is she fighting the need to push, perhaps because she is frightened or anxious? There are many possible reasons for this concern: fear of tearing; embarrassment about making a mess in the bed; concerns about the baby's health; social or family problems; acceptance of motherhood itself, to name a few. A gentle question such as "is there anything bothering you right now?" or "I get the feeling there is something on your mind that is holding you up" might encourage her to open up and express her fears. If she is able to voice her worries, avoid reassuring her — you cannot guarantee any particular outcome for her, and to suggest you can will undermine your credibility in her eyes. All you need do is acknowledge what she is saying — "I can see that is really bothering you" or "I guess we won't know the answer to that until the baby comes" or a similar empathetic response.

Perhaps she is not pushing because she doesn't need to — the baby is falling out easily!

Women who are upright often find they need to do less work, as gravity assists the baby to move down and they are not pushing uphill, as happens when she lying their backs.

You may be able to discover a physical reason to explain why she is not pushing, and offer an appropriate remedy. If her lack of effort reflects an emotional or psychological block, then some gentle questioning might help if there is time. On occasion, you may have to accept that she doesn't know herself why she is frightened of giving birth, and just offer her love, acceptance and physical support to help the baby out more easily without necessarily resorting to intervention.

Maintain a calm atmosphere. Check the baby's heartbeat unobtrusively, and be prepared to wait expectantly. If the woman is upright, gravity will speed the process and her need to push strenuously will be reduced. Enable her to work with her body, slowly and deliberately, by creating a relaxed, unhurried atmosphere.

Try not to make eye contact with her. Most women will have their eyes tightly closed during the birth, as they concentrate on pushing the baby out. Eye contact is very distracting, and makes others the focus of her attention, rather than enabling her to maintain close contact with the baby. Encouraging her to look in a mirror is also counterproductive — most women have never looked at their genital area in a mirror before, and even if they have, the unfamiliar sight that they will see at this point can be confusing. Instinctive behaviours are easier to access if the eyes are closed.

If she is unsure what is happening (and the huge, bulging feelings can be rather off-putting), encouraging her to touch the baby, while still inside her vagina, can enable her to make sense of the sensations she is feeling. Privacy, however, will again be important for this to happen — most women will feel very inhibited about putting their fingers into their vaginas if they feel they are "on view" to the world.

Positions for comfort

At this point, helping her to find an appropriate position will speed the second stage of labour. Lying down might feel comfortable, but when she tries to push, she may feel that her efforts are unproductive. Generally women like, even need, to be upright as this enables them to marshal their energies and use them effectively, assisted by gravity. Some possible positions are shown in figures 21, 22 and 23.

To increase her sense of privacy, and avoid unnecessary interventions (such as the giving of instructions), you could:

➡ Discourage her from getting onto the bed, as this will make her the centre of attention, and vulnerable to instruction, even coercion. Birth attendants are less likely to fall into the patterns of behaviour (also called habits) that appear automatically when they attend a woman giving birth on a bed. Some caregivers use "scripts" or standardised instructions, which not only depersonalises the birth for the woman, but turns birth into a mechanical event for the caregiver.

➡ Encourage her to stay on a mat on the floor. Women automatically assume upright positions when their feet are planted on the floor, and it will be much easier for them to alter their position when vertical.

➡ Make sure she is facing a wall or corner rather than the door, to reduce feelings of exposure.

➡ Enable her to use her partner for support. With her face buried against his chest and her eyes closed, her back will be towards the caregivers, making it harder for them to distract or coerce her through eye contact.

➡ A kneeling position will give her maximum control over the rate of descent of the baby (as she leans forward, gravity is reduced, thus slowing the baby's descent) and maximum privacy for her perineal area, which will be facing towards the floor.

➡ Position a mirror for your own use, either just in front of or just behind the woman, propped on a pillow or rolled towel to achieve the right angle (figure 24). This will eliminate the need for you to bend down or crawl around to see what is happening. When you can see the top of the baby's head in the mirror, kneel beside her, ready to receive the baby. If you have a bad back, sit on a footstool, to save bending.

➡ If she is squatting, be careful to offer no instructions, as any encouragement to push will add to the effects of gravity, and may make the birth too fast, resulting in tearing of the tissues. The burning sensation felt by

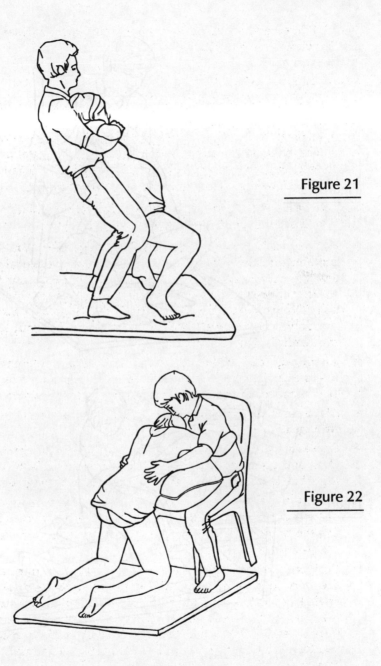

Figure 21

Figure 22

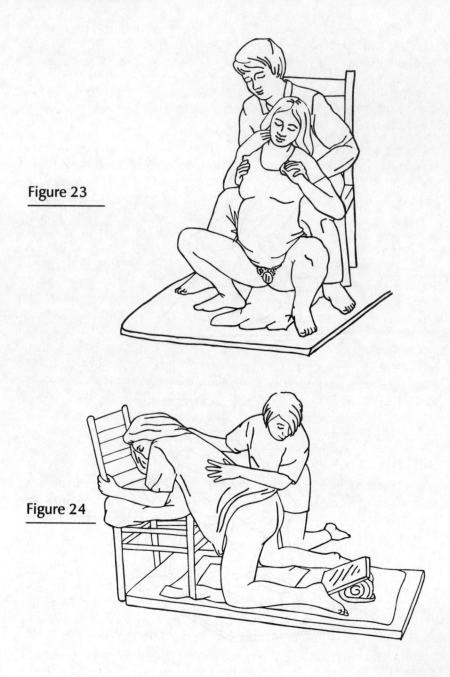

Figure 23

Figure 24

the woman as the head crowns is a clear signal to her that she should ease off pushing and allow time for stretching to occur. If you are talking to her as this happens she may be distracted from this internal message. If the baby appears to be coming very quickly, encouraging her forward onto her hands and knees will slow it down. Alternatively, you could say something like "take your time, you need the birth to be slow enough for the tissues to stretch around the baby".

As the second stage advances, there is little you need do, except maintain the calm setting, and listen to the baby's heartbeat as needed and prepare to receive the baby. There is no need to touch the perineum when the woman is upright as the skin stretches more evenly and the risk of tearing is much reduced.

Protecting the perineum

Suggestions for the pregnant woman

➡ Choose a midwife as your primary caregiver. There is abundant research supporting the fact that when a midwife assists at a birth, the perineum os less likely to be damaged. Doctors have a poor record in this regard.

➡ Perineal massage can increase the stretchiness of the tissues in the perineal area and prepare a woman for the sensations of crowning during the birth. The massage can be done daily in the last weeks of the pregnancy: oil your thumbs, place them inside the vagina and gently stretch sideways until a burning sensation is felt. Massage for a few minutes at that point. Although not a guarantee that the tissues will not tear during birth, massage can increase elasticity, soften tissues around a previous scar line (from an episiotomy) and reduce fear.

➡ During second stage, find a comfortable position that also feels effective in getting your baby born. It will most likely be an upright position, as this enables gravity to assist in the process.

➡ Once comfortable, maintain your position. If you find squatting works well, then you will need to rest your legs between the contractions, by either standing up or dropping forward onto your knees. This will avoid congestion in the vulval area due to constriction of the blood flow to the legs, caused by the pressure behind the knees and in the groin area. Puffy, oedematous tissues do not stretch very well, and may tear. You will also avoid cramps and aching legs if you rest between the contractions.

➡ Only push as you feel the need. The size of the baby and its position will determine the amount of effort required. Larger babies are harder to birth than smaller ones; second babies are easier than first babies; full term babies take more effort than premature babies or twins. The pushing urges come intermittently, and you should avoid holding your breath in between.

➡ Save your energy, by pushing with your body and at no other time. Avoid listening to onlookers or caregivers: an observer has no way of knowing just when you will be caught up in the overwhelming need to push, and they may instruct you to push unnecessarily, which is confusing and exhausting.

➡ Keep your eyes closed, so you can concentrate, and your ears closed, to avoid confusing instructions. No-one should be telling you when and how to push.

➡ When you feel the burning sensation, you will know that the baby is about to be born. If you are unsure about what is happening, try feeling the baby's head inside your vagina. Your natural instinct, when you feel this tight ring of fire, is to hold off from pushing. This is nature's way of encouraging you to slow down your effort momentarily while the tissues stretch to let the baby through.

➡ Take your time. There is no need to hurry second stage. You will know just how much effort is needed to bring your baby safely through the birth and you need time to enable to tissues to stretch and the baby needs time for its head to mould and to adjust to the changing pressures.

Some suggestions for caregivers

➡ Acquaint her with the information about the perineal tear rates of midwives compared with doctors. Make sure she knows the strategies for obtaining midwifery care during birth.

➡ Explain perineal massage techniques, and give her some written information about this.

➡ In second stage, assist her into an appropriate position of her choice.

➡ Protect her right to maintain this position. You will need advocacy skills for this, and perhaps techniques for conflict resolution, if she is to be protected from unnecessary intervention.

➡ Offer no instructions. Accept that she will be unable to avoid pushing when she is ready, and until that time, she needs to rest and conserve her energy.

➡ Avoid injecting local anaesthetic (just in case an episiotomy will be needed). The tissues will become puffy and less elastic and therefore more prone to tearing. She will also lose her biofeedback mechanism that encourages her to ease pushing at crowning.

➡ Keep you hands off the perineal area. The skin will be tight, tender and extremely sensitive. Touching it will cause her pain and she is likely to tense up, creating resistance rather than releasing the tissues. In the verti-

---

Physiologic third stage

The elements of a physiologic third stage include:

- No drugs (oxytocics, ARM, pethidine, epidurals etc.) earlier in the labour than may affect physiologic release of oxytocin in the third stage of labour.
- Placing the baby on the mat or mattress in front of the woman after it is born.
- Sitting the mother upright after the baby is born (unsupported).
- No injection of oxytocin.
- Giving the mother time to pick the baby up when she is ready.
- No distractions for the woman as she focuses on the baby.
- The woman supporting the baby in her arms (it is not lying on her tummy, pressing on the placenta).
- The cord not being clamped until after the pulsations have ceased (the cord may be left alone until after the placenta has arrived).
- If the cord is cut, the placental end being left to drain.
- The baby not being wrapped, but left skin to skin with the woman.
- The baby being encouraged to latch onto the nipple.
- When the contractions are again felt, the woman using her own expulsive efforts, together with gravity, to give birth to the placenta.
- No controlled cord traction.
- Continued suckling by the baby to encourage further uterine contractions.

---

cal position, the pressure from the baby's head is more evenly distributed around the opening, which reduces the risk of tearing as a result of the skin "ironing out" or being excessively thinned. The traditional midwifery skill of "guarding the perineum" stems from the need to protect the area when a woman is giving birth on her back — a very unnatural position that causes excessive perineal pressure towards the anus. This practice can be eliminated when women find their own instinctive upright positions for birth.

➡ Avoid massaging the area, as this is a gross invasion of privacy and very inhibiting for most women. The touching can also cause pain as the skin stretches which is counterproductive.

➡ There is no need to wash the area with sterile solutions, or oil it to keep it moist. The second show (often an indicator of imminent birth) and gushes of amniotic fluid that accompany the baby's arrival keep the area well lubricated. Creating sterility may override the baby's need for early exposure to the maternal bacterial flora essential for the beneficial colonisation of the baby's sterile intestinal system. The result may be late colonisation by unfamiliar, and perhaps dangerous bacteria, present in the birth environment.

If she is giving birth in a forward leaning position, then support the baby's head after it has been born and lift it up slightly against gravity as the shoulders arrive. This will encourage the anterior shoulder to come first. Once this has happened, lower the head and let gravity take over — the head will hang down and bring the posterior shoulder out. The main problem with birth in this position is that if the head is unsupported, the natural force of gravity will encourage it to hang downwards, causing the shoulders to come through together, rather than one at a time. In a bigger baby, this will cause excessive pressure on the anterior tissues and labial tears and grazes can result. These rarely need stitching but are very uncomfortable in the early post-partum period.

Warm compresses made from a folded washcloth wrung out in warm water and held against the perineum can be soothing if the stinging is very frightening for the woman and she is holding back.

Take your time. Patience will be rewarded with a woman who feel she has truly given birth using her own efforts and a baby whose arrival has been gentle and unhurried, and therefore less stressful.

After the baby is born

The minutes following the birth of the baby form a very special time for both mother and baby. The hormonal climate is unique, with both of them still under the influence of the hormones released during the labour. The presence of these hormones are essential elements in the attachment process between mother and baby (Lagercrantz 1986; Robertson 1994), and every effort must be made to avoid disturbing this unique relationship.

When the baby appears, you can:

➡ Receive the baby, and lower it onto the sterile sheet you have positioned under the mother. Make a quick visual assessment of the baby then withdraw, to encourage her to pick up her child when she is ready (figure 25). Avoid telling her the sex of the baby, offering loud congratulations, commenting on her prowess during the birth and other conversation. Peace, time on her own with her baby, and calm surroundings in which to explore the child and get her bearings are essential ingredients of the attachment process.

➡ Wait for the birth of the placenta, especially if no oxytocics have been used, provided there is no sign of excessive bleeding (much easier to see,

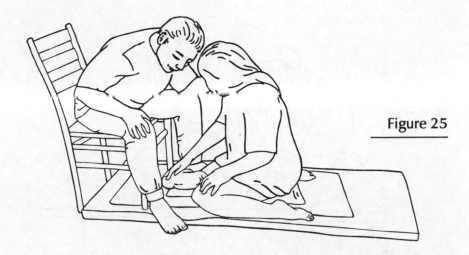

Figure 25

even from a distance, if she is sitting up). Cutting the cord can also be left until the placenta has arrived. Placental separation usually occurs within 30 minutes of the birth if there has been no hormonal disturbance or intervention earlier in the labour. Putting the baby to the breast will cause a surge of oxytocin to be released which will hastened separation, and the baby will be able to initiate the latching process if left with the mother, especially if she sits and holds the baby in her arms. The birth hormones enable instincts to work efficiently, enhancing rooting and latching in the baby, and nurturing and caretaking behaviours in the mother.

➡ Once the placenta has separated, the woman can kneel to enable the placenta to fall out (figure 26). There is no need to rush this, unless she is bleeding excessively, and if left alone, the placenta may even arrive on its own, as the mother breastfeeds her baby.

➡ Wait until after the first breastfeeding (probably an hour or more) before weighing and measuring the baby and carrying out other baby care tasks. Time alone for the new family is more important than getting everything cleaned up, the room shipshape and the paperwork completed.

➡ Find something for the father to do. Many men are overcome with joy, and some become quite noisy in their enthusiasm. If this happens their energies need to be directed away from the mother and baby so that breastfeeding can begin without disturbance. Phoning the grandparents (from a phone outside the birth room) or making a snack or cup of tea might be useful. Some men will be exhausted and emotional, and want a quiet time with the new mother and their baby, and this need must also be respected. Successful breastfeeding can hinge on taking advantage of

Figure 26

the unique hormonal interplay present in the hour following birth. The needs of the father may have to take a temporary second place to give the mother and baby the best chance to initiate lactation and the breastfeeding relationship.

Managing complications

So far, we have assumed that the woman in labour is having a straightforward, uncomplicated labour and is managing on her own, using her own inner resources and your thoughtful comfort measures. However, given the unpredictable nature of birth, it is useful to be prepared for those occasions when, for one reason or another, intervention is necessary and some kind of medical treatment is required. Sometimes, women themselves decide that they want additional help and opt for using pharmacological pain relief. In all of these cases, it is not necessary, or even desirable, to abandon all of the self help measures that the woman has found useful, and it is still possible to use many of them with great effect, to mitigate some of the disadvantages of using drugs and medical procedures.

Before exploring ways in which self-help measures can be combined with medical approaches, it is important to fully assess the situation, to determine if treatment is really required.

- Is the intervention really necessary?
- What alternatives have been tried?
- What are the expected benefits of the intervention?
- Are there any unwanted side effects that could arise?

- Do you have fully informed consent from the woman for this treatment?
- What would happen if nothing was done?

If, after carefully evaluating the answers to these questions the need for inter-vention is unequivocal, then it must be undertaken, with care and compas-sion. There are many things you, as a midwife, can do to reduce some of the side effects and minimise the trauma and discomfort that accompany many of these techniques. Many of the self-help suggestions in Chapter 6 such as posi-tioning, propping with pillows, massage, applying hot, wet towels, and offer-ing food and drink can be used alongside medical technology. It is not necessary to abandon them entirely, but using them can involve creativity and lateral thinking to adapt them to these new circumstances.

It is important to be aware of the risks and benefits of the treatments and to maintain vigilance over mother and baby once they have been applied. There is an increasing body of knowledge about the effects of drugs and interven-tions on the woman and her unborn baby, and keeping up with the expanding scientific evidence in this area is imperative. There is not scope in this book to canvass this research, and this information is available from many other sources (Enkin et al. 1994; Goer 1995; Wagner 1994; MIDIRS, The Cochrane Library, for example). Here, we shall concentrate on practical measures that midwives can use in conjunction with some common interventions and drugs.

Failure to progress

This is a diagnosis commonly made when women's labours do not follow a set pattern, and dilatation is slower than expected. The slowing of labour is a normal response to adrenalin in a woman's body and should not be seen as a "failure" on her part and the underlying hormonal actions are described in Chapter 5. The obvious response, when this situation occurs, is to look for the source of the anxiety or fear that is provoking the adrenalin, and to take steps to remove it. Some simple remedies that could be tried include:

➡ Give her privacy. Some time on her own, covering her up and lowering the lights to create intimacy will reduce the impact of other people and the surroundings.

➡ Change her environment. Moving her to a smaller room, or a different area (perhaps one that is more comfortable and less clinical) might help.

➡ Keep her warm. Long socks, a blanket or sheet and loose clothing will prevent the cooling that can trigger adrenalin.

➡ Offer her a warm water bath. Immersion automatically lowers blood pressure and calms panic, whilst creating privacy and a complete change of environment.

➡ If a bath is unavailable, try the shower.

➡ Address her fears, if she wants to express them. Some women know what is frightening them, others are unable to pinpoint the source of their anxiety. Avoid reassuring her — just listen as she talks.

➡ Remove strangers and anyone who is negative or anxious. The vibes created by these people can be very contagious, especially to a woman in labour who is especially sensitive.

➡ Hold her and provide close body contact. Some women like to be cuddled and to feel the strength and calmness of others through their touch.

➡ Reduce the impact of unwelcome sounds from nearby areas. The easiest way to do this is by offering her headphones on a portable cassette tape playing soothing music.

It takes time for these strategies to work. Adrenalin will gradually diminish and as it does both oxytocin and endorphins will begin to flow again. This may take an hour or more to achieve, so allow yourself this time before checking to see the results. As long as the mother and baby show no signs of medical problems, there is no need to rush into medical solutions, and it may be worthwhile spending time trying a number of strategies before deciding on intervention.

Induction and augmentation of labour

There are several ways of inducing labour (oxytocin drip, artificial rupture of the membranes, prostaglandin gel), with the most common trend being the use of prostaglandin gel to ripen the cervix and initiate labour through sensitising the uterus to the ever present oxytocin. Augmentation is usually achieved through either the use of an oxytocin drip or by rupturing the membranes (listed separately, below). Whatever procedure is being used, you can improve the woman's comfort by:

➡ Requesting that any drip be inserted in her arm rather than the back of her hand. A cannula in her hand will limit her ability to grasp or lean on her hand, both of which she may need to do when moving around.

➡ Providing a mobile drip stand so that she can walk around or get into the shower as needed for pain relief.

➡ Encouraging her to stay out of bed, and to adopt vertical positions. Labour induced using a drip is stronger and more painful than a physiological one, and she will need freedom of movement to help ease the additional pain. Almost all of the positions shown in Chapter 6 can be used while the woman is undergoing an induction or augmentation. Use some lateral thinking, and be creative with your adaptations.

➡ Making sure she has a good meal before the induction is started. The woman is often brought into the hospital for an induction early in the morning and may have had little food since the previous evening. This means she will be labouring with reduced stores of energy, and this will increase the likelihood of ketosis, fatigue and failure to progress. Regular fluids are also necessary through the labour.

➡ If a fetal monitor is to be used in conjunction with the drip, try some of the suggestions listed below to increase her comfort and mobility.

Fetal monitoring

Fetal monitors are often used routinely as part of the admission procedure when a woman arrives into the labour ward. The evidence supporting its use in this way is very shaky, and it has the potential for creating a clinical atmosphere while imposing subservience on perfectly normal, healthy women. When used to maintain continual surveillance on a baby showing signs of distress, the monitor can be a very helpful tool, but using it routinely, as a means of "baby-sitting" a labouring woman is risky and poor practice.

The impact of fetal monitors on a woman's comfort during labour can be reduced by:

➡ Not requiring the woman to lie down while it is being used. Indeed, a recumbent position may itself cause fetal distress, which the machine will then detect. Encourage her to stand or sit while it is in place.

➡ If she is moving around (pelvic rocking, for example) position her partner behind her so he can encircle her with his arms and hold the transducers in place. This will stop the transducers from falling off or moving and interrupting the trace.

➡ Intermittent monitoring, say for 10 minutes every hour, may be sufficient to chart the baby's well-being, especially if the monitor is only being used as an adjunct to an induction or epidural and there is no evidence of fetal distress.

➡ Attaching an electronic monitor will preclude the woman from using the bath or shower for relieving her pain. Hot, wet towels can still be applied, and with great success. Use them over the belts holding the transducers. Positioning the woman forward over beanbags and pillows will enable you to place the towels while the transducers are held in place by the pillows.

➡ A scalp electrode, whilst increasing the risk of infection in the baby, does give the woman more freedom of movement. It also gives a more accurate reading. A scalp electrode should only be used *after* the membranes have broken naturally, to avoid precipitating fetal distress from the extra pressure from the cervix against the baby's head following artificial rupture of the membranes.

➡ Telemetry units, available in some hospitals, enable the woman to walk around without being attached directly to the monitor. The woman must carry the battery pack and transmitter over her shoulder, which can be uncomfortable, but she can walk, sway, sit, and adopt many positions with much more ease. The monitor can be placed in the nursing station, to be supervised by the staff there, and this removes the tendency of the staff to focus on the machine rather than the woman sitting beside it in the labour ward. A disadvantage, however, is that the midwife can monitor the labour at a distance, and need not interact directly with the woman at all, although for some women, this enforced privacy may be more beneficial than having anxious midwives focusing on the machine at the bedside!

Artificial rupture of the membranes

Again, there is little scientific evidence to support the routine use of ARM. For the woman, rupturing her membranes exposes her to a sudden increase in the strength of contractions and the baby is exposed to the risk of infection. Whilst this is one procedure that midwives should question, if it has to be performed, you could help the woman by:

➡ Preparing her for the increased impact of the contractions. Remind her that her endorphin level will rise to help her cope with the added discomfort and pain, but this will need some time to develop.

➡ Encouraging her to remain upright. The added pressure from the contractions will be felt against the cervix and the tissues of the pelvic floor, rather than against bone and nerves as happens if she is lying down. Her ability to move freely in the upright position may increase her sense of security as she will be able to react freely to ease her pain — being recumbent while dealing with strong, hard contractions can increase the feeling of helplessness.

➡ Suggesting she adopt a knee/chest position might be useful for the first few contractions after the membranes are ruptured. This exaggerated forward position allows gravity to ease the baby away from the cervix which reduces the pressure on the baby's head, and decreases the pressure on the cervix. After the first few contractions following the ARM, the woman can gradually resume a more upright stance.

➡ Making sure she has adequate protection to catch the leaking amniotic fluid. These trickles of fluid can be very embarrassing and a source of anxiety. Thick sanitary pads inside her panties, or sitting her on the toilet or bedpan will ease her concerns.

➡ Having ruptured membranes does not preclude her from using the bath or shower to relieve her pain. The flotation effect of being in a bath may reduce the extra pressure on the cervix and ease her pain. The more localised heat provided by the shower may be useful in counteracting the pain of the contractions. Hot, wet towels may provide additional relief.

Epidural anaesthetics

This form of anaesthesia is the most reliable way of removing the pain in labour. A full epidural renders the woman unable to move, and increases the risk of side effects. Traditionally, women were required to remain in bed, recumbent at first, and then propped usually on their sides, whilst the epidural was working. The trend towards lighter anaesthetics injected in combination with narcotics gives women more freedom of movement, while reducing some of the risks. The greater mobility afforded by the newer combination anaesthetics means that women can move around more freely and take advantage of the beneficial effect of gravity in speeding up the labour. How much movement a woman is able to achieve will depend on a number of factors, and you can encourage her by:

➡ Sitting her up, with her legs over the edge of the bed and feet resting on a chair. She will need good back support to feel safe. She may be able to turn over into an all-fours position over a firm bean bag. You may need to lift the side rails on the bed to increase her feeling of safety. She may be able to walk around supported by her partner, if she has enough sensation in her feet and the narcotics have not made her feel dizzy.

➡ Avoiding using hot packs, hot, wet towels and similar forms of heat. Epidurals increase her temperature (an unwanted side effect), and cold, wet towels may be more welcome, especially on her legs and back.

➡ Offering her drinks, fruit-juice ice cubes to suck, or sweets. Although anaesthetists often request "nil by mouth" in case a general anaesthetic becomes necessary, there is no evidence that a woman is at increased risk of aspiration syndrome if she has been drinking and eating during labour. The few cases where aspiration has occurred during a general anaesthetic have been shown to be the result of poor anaesthetic technique (Broach & Newton 1988).

➡ Some hospitals are using patient-controlled epidurals, which have been shown to give better results, both in terms of patient satisfaction and lower overall exposure of mother and baby to the anaesthetic.

➡ Holding her in an upright position during second stage to enable gravity to bring the baby down.

If a person stands on either side of the bed, and she puts her arms around their necks (and they hold her around her back) she can be propped effectively to speed up progress by utilising gravity (figures 27 and 28). This is a useful position if she is exhausted, or has a reduced urge to push.

Pethidine (Meperidine)

The effects of this drug on a labouring woman is difficult to predict. Some will react strongly, and become very dopey and others will find pethidine has little effect on them. It is usually given in combination with other drugs to reduce the common side effects of nausea and vomiting. Working on the principle that it is always possible to give more, but impossible to reduce it once given, midwives can:

➡ Estimate the amount needed by calculating body weight and therefore dosage rates. This is standard practice in other areas of medicine, and can be applied in labour. Give the minimal dose and watch for reactions. A further top up can be used if necessary.

➡ Be wary of administering it towards the end of first stage. The increased risks to the baby are significant, both at birth (breathing difficulties etc.) and post-natally (for example, depressed sucking reflex, increased jaundice).

➡ Avoid using pethidine if the woman is in the bath or shower. If she reacts strongly to the drug, she could be at risk of falling over or slipping under the water!

➡ Physical support during second stage may be necessary if she is unable to push effectively. Propping or holding her in an upright position will enable gravity to assist the birth of the baby if her own efforts are unco-ordinated or ineffective.

➡ Position the baby on her tummy after it is born, to enable it to find the nipple by itself. Although a baby may be quite depressed if it has been exposed to pethidine, encouraging its innate instincts to find the nipple may be helpful in establishing breastfeeding. This could take an hour or more, and privacy, freedom from disturbance and supportive encouragement will be essential.

Nitrous oxide

Some women find that using the mask is a way of managing the strong contractions of transition. Others find it claustrophobic and confining. Some suggestions:

➡ A portable machine provides flexibility — it can be wheeled to the woman rather than her having to come to a fixed machine on the wall.

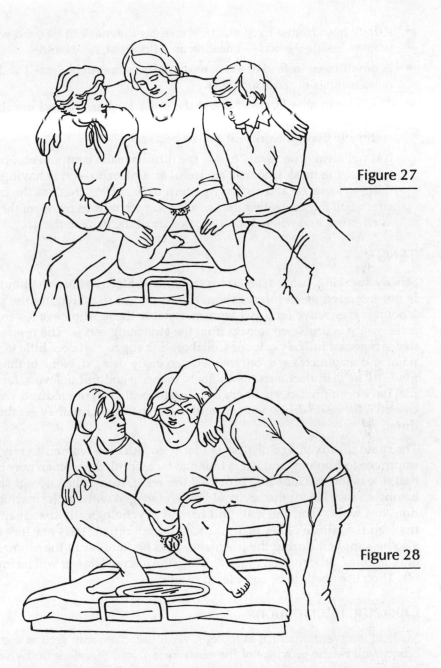

Figure 27

Figure 28

➠ A long hose from a fixed machine enables the mask to be used with the woman beside the bed — kneeling on a floormat, for example.

➠ A mouthpiece instead of a face mask reduces the rubber smell and eliminates feelings of claustrophobia.

➠ The woman should always hold the mask for herself, and use it as she needs. It should never be held in place by someone else. Good instruction on how to make it work will also ne necessary.

➠ It is not always necessary to use the nitrous oxide component. For some women, the mask is almost as useful as a placebo — it is having something to focus on and a steady pattern of breathing that has the calming effect. Full oxygen, rather than combined with nitrous oxide might be just as effective, and will reduce the exposure of the baby to the drug.

TENS

Strictly speaking, using TENS (Trans Cutaneous Electrical Nerve Stimulation) is not intended as an intervention, but as an aid to managing the pain in labour. It is effective for a few women, notably those who have severe backache, which is unrelated to pain from the stretching cervix. The research evidence reported in The Cochrane Collaboration suggests it does little to reduce pain, and may increase it, but that women enjoy using it. None of the claims made by its manufacturers (its ability to increase endorphin levels, for example) have been proven, and there is no evidence that its use reduces womens' overall reliance on drugs: women tend to use the TENS until they get their epidural.

The main disadvantage of TENS is that it encourages women to rely on an unproven technology, and if it is found to be helpful, the woman may believe that it was the machine that provided the relief, rather than accept she was having an easy labour that she could have managed without the machine. If it does not work, then she may find herself psychologically disadvantaged, through the failure of her main source of preparation. TENS machines must also be supplied during the pregnancy and be familiar to the woman, and once in place, other options such as using the bath or shower will be impossible. Their use needs to be considered carefully.

Obstetric interventions

Medical interventions such as forceps, ventouse, caesarean section and episiotomy will be the province of the obstetrician, and therefore midwives will have fewer opportunities to work with women in these circumstances. However, there are still important ways for midwives to assist, particularly in dealing with the emotions and trauma that can arise in a crisis.

➡ Act as an interpreter for the woman and her partner. Explain what is happening, the details of the procedure and what she may feel. Try to be brief, honest and straightforward, using simple language whilst avoiding emotional overtones.

➡ Acknowledge her feelings, worries and concerns. Answer her questions. She needs you as an ally and you are the person she knows and trusts, having spent time with her during the labour. Avoid reassurance ("I'm sure the baby will be fine") as this will have a hollow ring, and she will know that you are mouthing platitudes. You could lose your credibility by making these kinds of false, though well-meaning, statements.

➡ Make sure that she sees her baby as soon as possible. Take photographs of the baby, particularly after a caesarean section under a general anaesthetic. She may not remember holding the baby, and a photograph will reinforce her memory and prove she did hold her baby straight away.

➡ Try to put the baby to the breast immediately after the birth. Of course, this will depend on the baby's condition, but there will be many times when the intervention was carried out for reasons to do with the woman rather than her child, and the baby will be quite well and able to breastfeed. You may need to hold the baby for her, and involve the partner. Contact between the mother and her baby, and breastfeeding in the first hour after birth are significant factors in establishing successful lactation.

➡ Make sure that the partner is not excluded when a medical intervention is needed. If he is present, and can see what is being done (and it is being explained to him) he will be satisfied that everything possible was attempted in the circumstances. This might be traumatic (and will need careful de-briefing) but it can be useful in helping him to come to terms with the eventual outcome. He is also better equipped to explain to his partner what happened, and this may be crucial in helping her to accept the outcome as well. Involving parents in this way is an important step in reducing the chance of later litigation.

These suggestions for incorporating self-help and active birth principles into the management of high risk labour are just a beginning, and are designed to stimulate your creative thinking. It could be argued that when a medical emergency occurs or obstetric intervention is essential, a midwife, with her philosophy of keeping birth normal, is an essential member of the team, to help keep the birth in perspective, and to make the outcome as "human" as possible. Your midwifery touch may provide the difference between a medicalised birth and a humanised birth in difficult circumstances. Yet another challenge for the dedicated midwife!

115

References

Broach J & Newton N 1988, 'Food and beverages in labour. Part II: The effects of cessation of oral intake during labour', *Birth*, vol. 15, pp. 88–92.

Caldeyro-Barcia R. 1979, 'The Influence of maternal bearing-down efforts during second stage on fetal well-being', *Birth*, vol. 6, no. 1.

Enkin M, Kierse M., Renfrew M. & Neilson J 1994, *A Guide to Effective Care in Pregnancy and Childbirth*, Oxford University Press, London.

Fawcett M. 1993, *Aromatherapy for Pregnancy and Childbirth*, Element Books, London.

Goer H. 1995, *Obstetric Myths versus Research Realities*, Bergin & Garvey, USA.

Hannah M. et al. 1996, 'Induction of labour compared with expectant management for prelabour rupture of membranes at term', *New England Journal of Medicine*, vol. 334, no. 16, pp. 1005–10.

Jacobsen B et al. 1988, 'Obstetric pain medication and eventual adult amphetamine addiction in offspring', *Acta Obstet Gynecol Scand*, vol. 67, pp. 677–81.

Jacobsen B et al. 1990, 'Opiate addiction in adult offspring through possible imprinting after obstetric treatment', *B Med J*, vol. 301, pp. 1067–70.

Kanto I. 1984, 'Obstetric analgesia, pharmacokinetics and its relation to neonatal behavioural and adaptive functions', *Biological Research in Pregnancy*, vol. 5, pp. 23–35.

Kuhnert B. et al. 1985, 'Disposition of meperidine and normeperidine following multiple doses during labour: II Fetus and neonate', *Am J Obstet Gynecol*, vol. 151, pp. 410–15.

Lagercrantz H. & Slotkin T. 1986, 'The "stress" of being born', *Scientific American*, April, pp. 100–107.

Nathanielsz P. 1994, *A Time to be born*, Oxford University Press, UK.

Righard L & Shnider S. 1990, 'Effect of delivery room routines on success of first breast feed', *Lancet*, vol. 336, pp. 1105–07.

Robertson A. 1994, *Empowering Women — Teaching active birth in the 90s*, ACE Graphics, Sydney.

—— 1994, *Preparing for Birth*, ACE Graphics, Sydney.

Rosenblatt D. et al. 1981, 'The influence of maternal analgesia on neonatal behaviour: II Epidural Bupivacane', *Br J Obstet Gynaecol*, vol. 88, pp. 407–17.

Sepkoski C., Lester B., Ostheimer G. & Brazelton T. 1992, 'The effects of maternal epidural anesthesia on neonatal behaviour during the first month', *Developmental Medicine and Child Neurology*, vol. 34, pp. 1072–1080.

Thorp J. et al. 1993, 'The effect of intrapartum epidural analgesia on nulliparous labour: A randomised, controlled, prospective trial', *Am J Obstet Gynecol*, vol. 169, pp. 851–8.

Tiran D. 1996, *Aromatherapy in Midwifery Practice*, Bailliere Tindall, London.

Tiran D. & Mack S. 1995, *Complementary Therapies for Pregnancy and Childbirth*, Bailliere Tindall, London.

Wagner M. 1994, *Pursuing the Birth Machine*, ACE Graphics, Sydney.

Wesson N. 1995, *Alternative Maternity*, Macdonald Optima, London.

Chapter 7

SUPPORTING PARTNERS

Being invited to accompany a woman on her journey through birth is one of the most exciting and humbling experiences in life. It is both an honour and a privilege, and presents an opportunity for personal growth and insight unique in our lives. The role of support person requires sensitivity and love, whilst at the same time demanding physical stamina and endurance, a heady mix that can leave those involved with a confusing mixture of emotions and symptoms after it is all over: elation, relief, euphoria, exhaustion, intense muscle fatigue, and body aches to name a few.

In discussing the role of support people, these comments reflect the view that whoever is with the woman during labour and birth can be considered a "support person", and whilst this term is generally applied to the father of the baby, in effect the woman's chosen companions all form part of her support team, including the midwife, doctor, paediatrician and any other professional attendants who may be present. Therefore, the approach used here is to consider the term "support person" as generic, with the observations and suggestions being equally applied to any person who is going to be present. Fathers do have particular needs, however, and these will be addressed separately.

Support people often accept the invitation to be at a birth without fully realising what the role involves. First time fathers may just expect to be there, with little thought about what this might entail. Many women often assume the father of their baby will be present to nurture, guide and offer comfort through the labour, especially in today's society where fathers are almost expected to attend. Others want their man to witness the birth as a way of ensuring a closeness to the baby and effective bonding as a parent. For other expectant mothers, the thought of having one's sexual partner present is a strange and uncomfortable thought, and a female companion is sought as a labour companion. Other people may see the invitation as a way to witness a birth and find out what happens when a baby is born.

There is much discussion, even debate over who *should* be present at birth as labour companions. This discussion often centres on the people the woman is allowed to bring with her — the number of hospital staff allowed or even required to be in attendance being rarely questioned. This issue does not arise when the baby is born at home, since it is well understood that the mother is entitled to invite anyone she pleases into her home. In this setting, it is the number of professional attendants who are *allowed* to be present that is considered — a neat reversal of the situation in hospital and a reflection on the innate social importance of birth.

In the event, it is the woman's place to decide whom she would like to have as companions and it is up to her to issue the invitations. Only she can know who would be best suited to offering her comfort and protection, and in whose presence can feel uninhibited and safe. These issues of safety, protection and privacy need to be explored in detail during the pregnancy, and a midwife can present them for consideration during pre-natal visits. One effect of having support people present is the potential for the invasion of a woman's personal space. Some women find this a comfort, feeling cocooned by the close proximity of other caring people. Others may find it stifling and even embarrassing to have others share the intimacy of natural birth behaviours. Until the labour begins it will be impossible for a woman to know just what will feel right for her, so flexibility rather than rigid planning is essential.

Having extra people, carefully chosen from family or friends, can be helpful for women giving birth in hospitals. This is the ultimate way of bringing useful items from home to help create a familiar environment — having significant others nearby is a powerful reminder of the social importance of birth, and they can enable women to feel safer in alien surroundings.

Choosing support people

Women need to consider carefully whom they would like to invite to their labours. Traditionally, other close female relatives were present, to help build family ties through the bonding that occurs between the baby and those present at the birth. This would have been important on those rare occasions when the mother died or was unable to care for her baby — there were other women who felt sufficiently connected to the baby to take over the mother's role and therefore ensure the child's survival. These days, the bonding of those present at birth can help overcome some of the isolation experienced by westernised families who have few family social supports available locally. Encouraging a woman to bring in her close friends may also help to re-create the community links between families and help demystify birth amongst women in our society. The birth of a baby was always a time for rejoicing and celebration, and one of the saddest outcomes resulting from the supplanting of birth from the home into the hospital has been the loss of this opportunity. Births are celebrated in hospitals in a ritualised, formal way (restricted visiting, a bunch of flowers, a box of chocolates, a brief cuddle of the baby), and spontaneous family celebrations are seen to be inappropriate. No champagne, feasts or singing here!

Women may need time to consider whom they could invite to the birth, especially if it is to take place in the hospital. Several factors need to be addressed, including the support person's:

- Availability, especially for a long labour.
- Willingness to be there and to be actively involved before, during and after the birth.
- Feelings about birth, especially acceptance of birth as a normal event. Personal experiences, or a known fear of blood or hospitals, for example, may affect the comfort level of support people.
- Sensitivity and insight. Common sense is a useful trait, as is unshockability!
- Comfort with nakedness, bodily functions and uninhibited behaviour (birth can feel very sexy at times).
- Willingness to leave if appropriate or requested by the mother.

Women may decide to select several companions and to leave the final decision about who is to be invited until labour begins. At that time, the heightened sensitivity engendered by the labour hormones can sharpen her awareness of potential supporters' strengths and weaknesses and make it easier for her to decide who should be contacted. It is helpful if potential supporters are aware that their invitation is dependent on the woman's feelings at the time, and if they are accepting of her decision. Many women find labour easier to manage if they are on their own, for example, and may want companions to keep their distance, perhaps nearby, in another room. Women should not be left alone to labour, but being by themselves, with others close by, can have a powerful effect on the speed of birth, since this approach will ensure few distractions or disturbances of the hormones.

During the pregnancy

The commitment to support a woman in labour ideally includes being available for her during the pre-natal period as well as after the baby is born. Some people see the invitation to attend a birth as a chance to see a baby born, and a way to fulfil their own curiosity or needs. They may not understand that the role could involve active participation and perhaps assistance.

Some discussion during the pregnancy with potential support people, including the father (as described below) can help to clarify perceptions and expectations and improve communication between those involved. Sometimes the woman will choose a person who has had previous experience of birth (her mother, for example) and it is important to provide an opportunity for this person to fully debrief her own birth(s) before attending another woman during labour. Unresolved grief, anxieties, even unanswered questions can all develop into personal dramas that can block effective care for another woman during birth. The midwife is an ideal person to spend some time debriefing prospective labour companions, listening to their stories, answering questions, even facilitating healing in some circumstances. A special time set aside for this purpose can reduce future trauma especially if the consultation can take place in private, away from the pregnant woman.

The father may have particular concerns as well. Since men have only been present at births for the to last 25 years or so, they don't have older male relatives in whom they can confide or with whom they can discuss the practicalities of being present during birth. The male "macho" image can also hinder frank discussion among peers, and often the chance to talk about mutual concerns with friends is just not available. A private conversation with a midwife might also be in order for the fathers, to explore anxieties, answer specific questions and generally acknowledge his special perspective and needs.

Some of these issues can also be raised in pre-natal classes. Well planned and presented classes include discussion and information directed primarily at fathers, and provide opportunities for the men in the group to share and work together on issues of specific importance to their needs. Some childbirth educators provide a separate session just for the men alone, perhaps with a male group leader.

Inviting other people who may form part of the support team at the birth to attend pre-natal classes together with the woman and her partner is a very sound strategy. The woman is able to assess the willingness of her chosen friends to take on the broader commitment; she is able to experience their sensitivity, creativity and ability to use common sense in the practical sessions (especially those focusing on self-help measure in labour, for example); she can hear them talk about their beliefs and values surrounding births which can give her insights into attitudes that may be helpful or unhelpful in labour. The "team" learn more about each others' skills and develop ways of working together towards a common goal. Feeling equipped with specific tasks and clearly defined goals can not only increase the ability of supporters to assist, but also reduce fears centred around "what will I do to help?".

Visiting the labour ward, if the baby is to be born in a hospital is also useful for labour companions. They can join a regular tour, or perhaps arrange to visit with the pregnant woman privately. An orientation to the unit, especially one that focuses on what the team can do to help will increase their confidence. It is difficult for them to support a labouring woman in her bid to be independent and autonomous if they feel they are not welcome or comfortable in the hospital environment themselves. They need to find out:

- Where they can get drinks, ice or light snacks for the labouring woman. The kitchen area should not be off limits to them.
- Where the bedpans are kept.
- Where extra pillows, bean bags, floor mats, sheets, towels and hot packs can be obtained.
- The location of a variety of simple chairs available for women to use during labour,
- How to darken the room, operate blinds, move furniture (especially the bed) within the room to make more space.
- What is kept in the drawers in the labour room: extra sanitary pads, vomit bowls, plastic cups, flexible straws, inco pads (large absorbent pads with plastic on one side).
- Where the bathroom facilities are located, should the labouring woman wish to use the toilet, shower or bath.
- Where they can obtain food and drink for themselves.
- Which toilet is designated for visitor use.
- Disposal arrangements for rubbish.
- The telephone available for their use during labour and after the birth.
- How to access the unit after hours, if a different entrance is used during night time hours.

The most practical way of covering this information is to set up a role play, with the woman practising her comfort positions and various labour scenarios together with her support team, while they are visiting the labour ward area. A "dress rehearsal" of this kind will empower those concerned by thoroughly familiarising them with the unit's facilities. In addition, the support of the midwife in facilitating this practice session gives a strong message about the unit's flexibility and encouragement of parents to take responsibility for their own comfort: it encourages independence rather than dependence. If parents know how to take care of themselves during the labour and birth, then they will be less likely to be constantly leaning on the midwifery staff for guidance and permission. Giving responsibility in this way to the parents is a fine acknowledgment of their capabilities and a firm demonstration of trust. It not only helps to demystify hospital equipment and paraphernalia, it makes a statement about the hospital's commitment to accessibility and service. A final bonus is that the midwifery staff, through encouraging creative and practical labour ward tours that actually involve the participants, have a chance to demonstrate their own skills and openness towards individualised birth experiences based on women's needs rather than hospital protocols. It is a neat and subtle way of selling midwifery! There is more about labour ward tours in Chapter 9.

Another strategy for addressing the perceived roles of the intended birth companions is for the whole team to have a structured discussion about the plan for labour. Each person writes down what they see themselves doing during the labour and what they see every other person doing. When this is completed, the lists are discussed, and every one can compare what they saw themselves doing with what other people's expectations are of them. Negotiation can then take place if the differences are significant. For example, the expectant mother might say that apart from having the baby, her role will be to tell everyone else what she needs, and to enlist the childbirth educator (who has been invited to attend) as her advocate and liaison person with the staff. The father on the other hand, might feel that it is his role to determine what she needs and to act as her advocate. The mother might reply that she just wants him to be there to give comfort and that the educator is better equipped to talk with staff, if necessary. The educator might have considered her role to include providing comfort as needed and to support the father as advocate, since she does not see herself in that role. Round table discussion may well follow in which the roles are redefined and clarified to everyone's satisfaction. It is better to have this kind of discussion before labour starts, to reduce the risks of misunderstandings occurring during the birth itself.

During labour

Another role for the midwife during labour is caring for the support team. If they are happy and relaxed, the woman will labour better, especially those women who seem at times to be more focused on their partner's needs rather than on their own. We have all seen women in labour anxiously monitoring their partner's comfort and fussing over his needs in between her own strong contractions! You can help enormously in this situation by paying attention to the support people, giving them a break, arranging for a hot drink etc. — whatever seems necessary to relieve her concern of their welfare. With her mind at ease, she can get on with the work of giving birth, knowing that her companions are well cared for.

There can be no doubt that birth companions find the long hours of labour draining and exhausting. While the labouring woman has her hormones to assist her (easing the pain, reducing external awareness, obscuring the passage of time) those with her will be very aware of the hours dragging on and their own growing fatigue. This is especially true of the middle phases of first stage, when the labour is well established and the contractions seem to stay much the same for many hours. The changes that herald transition can come as quite a relief from the monotony of one contraction after another, particularly when the room is quiet and dark, the woman is very self-absorbed and a rhythmic pattern of back rubbing or hot towel application has been quietly established. Everyone sinks into a kind of torpor — a wonderful way to labour, and very productive, yet the mesmeric action can increase feelings of fatigue in the assistants. It is important for them to take time out to go to the toilet, get a breath of fresh air, have a snack and even have a nap. Very few support people feel like leaving a woman in this state, however, unless they can be absolutely certain that in their absence the back rubbing will continue exactly as established, the hot towels will continue to be applied just as she wants and that no-one will take advantage of the situation to impose unwanted or unnecessary interventions. Coming back to find that a midwife has insisted on an internal examination and then given pethidine in response to the woman's increased pain (due to moving her to the bed), is devastating for a support person, who will be very wary of the midwife after that. Any trust that had been established with hospital staff will evaporate and the support person is likely to maintain a watchful vigilance as a protector, at the expense of their own needs.

The needs of fathers

For the father of the baby, extra pressures apply when the baby is born in a hospital. It is often assumed that he will provide comfort and practical assistance, take responsibility, act as a go-between on occasion between his partner and the staff and be an advocate when she is unable to take charge herself. As well, he is expected to be emotionally involved with her and the baby and to put his own feelings aside so he can be strong for her. In most cases, however, he will have no idea of the hospital rules and protocols, have never met the staff of the unit, be unfamiliar with the medical jargon and the actual birth process and have a whole range of potential emotions that no-one seems aware of or concerned about. In addition, his partner may be going through a scary looking birth process, in pain at times, and he can be torn between wanting to facilitate the birth she desires yet not wanting either her or the baby to suffer. It is an unenviable position, made more difficult because he has often had inadequate preparation and has few outlets for venting his own feelings.

What can a midwife do to help this man carry out his natural protective role and gain the maximum benefits from being present at the birth of his baby? Some possible ideas:

➡ Spend some time talking to the father during the labour. There will be times when the woman is quite comfortable on her own, and you can turn your attention to his physical and emotional needs.

➡ Make sure he knows where he can get hot drinks, a snack or even a meal. In many hospitals, staff offer the meal that has been ordered for her (she is an in-patient and therefore entitled to a meal, even if it is unlikely that she will want to eat it) to her partner. In other hospitals, a system is used where substantial snacks for the fathers such as sandwiches, fruit and simple desserts are kept in a fridge. These arrangements are very useful when no other source of food is available, such as in the middle of the night, when the cafeteria or snack bar in the hospital is closed.

➡ Acknowledge his feelings. Enable him to voice his concerns, ask questions and share his emotions. Once again, your listening skills will be an asset in this process.

➡ Find somewhere where he can have a sleep. If she is labouring during the night, he may have come straight from work to the hospital and been tired before he started supporting her. If the woman is comfortable on a mat on the floor, perhaps he can use the labour room bed. Some labour wards have recliner rocker chairs that fathers find comfortable for napping. An unoccupied waiting room might have space for a mat on the floor for him to lie on. A blanket and pillow will help him sleep.

➡ Encourage him to join her in the shower or bath (if there is room) when she is using the hot water for pain relief. The warm water will calm and refresh him too. He can strip down to his underpants (if he has a spare pair) or be naked (this will ensure privacy, at least!).

➡ Explain what is happening and what he can expect to see as the labour develops. Some warning in advance of what transition may be like may reduce his shock and concern later on. He will naturally be anxious about anything that appears to be making labour worse for her, so be particularly careful to explain all medical procedures that might be used, before they begin.

➡ Don't force him to do more than he wants. If he wants to stay outside, make him feel comfortable about this decision. Be sensitive to the impact that the birth may be having and find ways of lessening its effects on him. For example, have him at the head of the bed if an episiotomy is to be done — watching someone cutting his partner's vagina could be very traumatic for many men. Include him in the caesarean section if he is willing to be there. Discuss what will happen and provide a running description as the surgery takes place. A place to sit, whilst feeling involved, can reduce natural anxiety.

➡ Be aware that in some cultures men are considered inappropriate birth companions for women. A generation ago it was uncommon for men to be involved in any births, and now there seems to be a general expectation that the father will, or even should, be present for the birth. These expectations can be unfair on both men and women, some of whom have very definite preferences about who should be at the birth. Discussion about this issue in advance and respect for the final decision is vital.

➡ Debrief the father after the birth. Women are often given an opportunity to talk to the midwife after the birth, but the fathers are rarely included. Many men will have on-going feelings that need to be resolved. Some may have been severely traumatised, especially if an emergency required medical heroics to save the baby, or mother. Others may have been shocked by the process, or any of the events that surrounded the labour — all these need airing if the man is to begin resolving the issues in his mind. If this doesn't happen, then they may emerge in the next pregnancy and influence events in the next labour.

➡ Avoid make assumptions about the degree or quality of the support he is offering. People react in different ways to being present during labour, and the relationship that already exists between the woman and her partner will continue as usual, even though she is labouring. For example, some couples argue and bicker, right between the contractions; whereas another woman might prefer to get on with labour by herself while her partner sits on a chair on the other side of the room reading the paper, apparently uninterested. Try to avoid putting your own interpretations on these scenarios — these people may naturally behave like this and be comfortable with this level of interaction. Labour will not necessarily change this!

Other issues concerning support people

Occasionally, the woman in labour decides to bring a number of relatives and friends into the hospital with her. She may have invited them herself, or they may have arrived as "uninvited guests" who nevertheless feel they want or even need to be involved with the birth. A social gathering can develop, with the woman surrounded by her friends and relatives, all chatting and interacting with each other and the woman. This unintentional invasion can not only disturb her privacy, it can make concentration difficult, slowing labour and making it less productive. The alert midwife will notice what is happening and be aware that something needs to be done for the labour to regain strength. There are a number of possible solutions, and some preventative measures that can be considered. Before the labour begins:

➡ The woman can be asked to give the staff a list of those people she has invited. Name tags could even be prepared, so that when the guests arrive, those who have invitations from the woman are clearly identified. Having name tags may seem formal, however they are a clear indication that the staff are ready for the visitors and this can been seen as a welcoming gesture.

➡ A discussion with the woman about the importance of carefully choosing support people provides an opportunity to review the physiology of labour and the impact of disturbance and distraction on her hormonal balance. One way to simplify this is to point out that she will need to be very comfortable being naked in front of her birth companions and may find herself vomiting, using a bedpan or passing wind in their company. This graphic (but gently described) picture will help her get the message.

➡ Hospital protocol sometimes insists that intended support people visit the labour ward to familiarise themselves with what will happen and what is expected of them in this role.

During the labour, if the "team" seem to be interrupting rather than enhancing the labour, there are other measures that can ease the situation:

➡ Asking the additional helpers to leave or take a meal break might work. An explanation, put sympathetically yet clearly that the extra people are unintentionally slowing her labour, may do the trick. A roster could be decided amongst themselves, although the woman may find that a changing team of assistants is counterproductive as well.

➡ Giving each member of the group a specific task can involve people in contributing to the labour rather than just socialising. Midwives can usually find several small jobs that need to be done, and people often liked to be asked to help. Sometimes their idle chatter is really a cover for embarrassment at not knowing what is expected of them or being unsure how they could actually assist.

➡ If the guests are unwilling to leave (and some feel very protective — "I came here to be with my daughter/sister/friend and I am going to stay right till the end!") it might be simpler to take the woman away to another area. It is easy to find a simple, acceptable excuse, such as her need to go to the toilet, and the visitors will usually accept her absence in these circumstances quite well, and will wait quite happily until she gets back. You can use this separation as an opportunity to check how the woman feels about the extra people, and if she is unhappy with their presence, you can offer to make her comfortable in the toilet or bathroom for a time, to give her some peace and privacy.

It is important not to make assumptions about the effect a woman's support team is having on her. Take time to absorb the situation, evaluate the interactions and assess their impact. Always check out your conclusions with the woman herself, preferably in private. It is easy to accidentally impose your own values in these situations, which may be harmful. For example, in some cultures it is very acceptable to have a number of woman friends present, whose role may seem to be one of deliberate distraction from the task in hand (the labour), but who nevertheless, by their apparent casual indifference, create a feeling of normalcy about giving birth. Breaking up this kind of gathering could have the opposite effect of what was intended, and rather than increase her feeling of security, the labouring woman may feel suddenly isolated, frightened and alone.

Siblings

For some families, the inclusion of the other children at the birth of a sibling is an important family event. Having prepared for the new baby together, planned for celebrating its arrival, even jointly deciding on a name, means that excluding the other children from the birth would be unthinkable. Other families take a different approach, and many children don't want to be at the birth at all (yukky!). There are many variations, and a flexible system that encourages the involvement of other children on request is necessary if the maternity service is to meet the needs of all expectant families in the community.

There is little research into the effects of being at a birth on siblings. Much anecdotal evidence supports the idea, as long as the children want to be present, have been well prepared and have their own known carer with them. This last point is vital for young children, who need someone other than mummy or daddy available at all times to take care of their needs, which will vary according to their age. Children under three years have fewer language skills so it can be harder to recognise what they are feeling or needing. They do have expressive faces, however, and display their emotions freely — what you see is generally what you get! Older children have learned to control their emotions to some extent, and can therefore be harder to "read" regarding their reactions to what is happening around them. They too need someone available to care for them, preferably someone who can talk freely and comfortably about birth and who knows the child(ren) well enough to have a good rapport with them. Teenage children present another challenge. They are often wrestling with their own sexuality and may have trouble accepting the explicitness and frankness of birth. All children will have residual feelings about seeing the baby born and all will need the opportunity to debrief and assimilate what they have seen. Talking the events over later with the midwife would be a helpful step in this process.

The presence of siblings at a home birth presents few problems, since the environment is familiar, the children have their own individual space where they can withdraw if they want, and the potential disruption to normal family routines is minimal. They will still need their own carer, and the option of being present or not. Talking about it all afterwards will be necessary to answer any questions and sort out any feelings they have about the labour and birth.

Taking siblings to a hospital presents special challenges. If the siblings are young (under 5 years old, for example) then there are special considerations: how can the child be amused if the labour is long? Will it be possible for the child to sleep somewhere if necessary? Is there a lounge area, waiting room or similar space where the child can be entertained away from the labour room itself? Older children are more capable of managing missed sleep and restrictions on their movements, but they still need to be able to get away if desired. Another practical point is whether the child(ren) can be woken from their sleep and be able to function quickly as the family makes speedy preparations for going to the hospital in the middle of the night. If waking children in this way is likely to result in grumpy or unco-operative behaviour, then perhaps leaving them asleep at home and calling in an emergency babysitter would be a better solution.

If parents are considering including their other child(ren) in the birth of the new sibling, some basic issues must be addressed:

➡ Do the child(ren) really want to be present? Have they expressed this desire themselves, spontaneously? If not, are they being pushed to do something they really don't want to do?

➡ The presence of other children is distracting for a woman in labour. Part of her attention will always be centring on what the child is doing and how they are reacting (mothers always have part of their mind focused on their children at all times) and this can be a powerful inhibitor of labour. There are some mothers who will, however, relax more successfully if they know that their other children are still safely within sight, particularly if they have uncertain baby sitters or few social supports for the family.

➡ Flexibility will be required in both the planning and implementation. Circumstances may dictate a rapid change of plans: the baby may be coming too fast to drop the other siblings off at a babysitter on the way; the other child may be sick and therefore unable to cope; children may be in school and unable to be brought home in time; someone (the mother/father/child) may change their mind at the last moment. Contingency plans are necessary to cover many possible scenarios and an open mind will be needed right up to the birth. It can be a total surprise to see how it all works out.

➡ Good preparation is essential. Children need to be comfortable with the sights, sounds and even smells of labour, and this can be achieved through story books, watching carefully selected videos and playing with dolls. There is quite a range of suitable sibling preparation materials available these days, and your local childbirth educator should be able to provide some resources. If the family are generally modest (even with younger children) and have not discussed sexual issues, then the nakedness and raw emotions of birth may be very frightening for the unprepared child.

➡ A child's "goody bag" with drinks, snacks, favourite comforter, toys, change of clothes (and spare nappies etc. for little children) needs to be ready well in advance.

These suggestions cover the basic issues surrounding having siblings present at the birth. Children are often delighted at seeing their brother or sister born, and can often be much more matter-of-fact about birth than adults. As it is difficult to predict just how children will react. Making assumptions can be risky — being open to the idea and exploring the possibilities can open up new lines of communication within the family which at the very least, brings its own rewards. Involving children can prevent the creation of scary impressions about birth and is another way of broadening community education. As a midwife, you need to be welcoming of the idea and open to its possibilities. Seeing birth through children's eyes is an impressive experience!

Chapter 8

ACTING AS AN ADVOCATE

It is generally accepted that the needs of women should be central to all policies concerning childbirth and that they should be directly involved in all decisions that affect their care. This is easier said than done, and there are many reasons why women feel disenfranchised within the health care system. For some there will obvious problems such as language barriers and culturally inappropriate services, for others, the inflexibility of the system will make it difficult for women to fully participate in the services that do exist. These issues come to a head in maternity care, where the medical model clashes with social needs, leaving women in a kind of limbo, not knowing just how they should, or can, fit in.

Since midwives have a pivotal role in the provision of maternity care, acting as an advocate for women, as well as a woman's advocate is almost a necessity, given the current situation. There is a curious attitude prevailing in some quarters, related to the push for patient's rights and informed consent from the consumers of health services. Women are now being exhorted to "Tell us what you want — it's your birth, and your experience. You must inform us of you wishes and we will carry them out!". Good advice — if it were possible. In order to make an informed decision, women must have information, the ability to choose, time to consider the issue, and support for the option chosen. These factors are rarely provided, especially all together, and women are left to struggle in a fog of confusion. If they make a poor decision, or make no decision (perhaps because they were unable to sort out what was required) then there is a tendency to blame the victim, with almost a cry of triumph: "See, women can't decide, we know best after all". The ambivalence of the health system's attitude towards autonomy (as exemplified in the double

131

standards described on page 13) is also a major factor in the denial of patient's rights and the setting up of conflict between doctors and midwives.

Many women do find their way through the health care maze if they are persistent and have a strong sense of identity, plus skills in negotiation and the ability to be assertive. For most, the very hormones of pregnancy mitigate against these kinds of actions — women are seeking protection, guidance, care and nurture at this time in their lives. This must not be viewed as a weakness, but a biological necessity, designed to ensure that women are looked after, and that they receive solicitous attention, important factors in maintaining the health of mother and baby. Unfortunately, these natural tendencies of women are often exploited and used against them, and there are many examples of emotional blackmail, coercion and plain bullying that could be described by anyone working in maternity care.

One lighthouse in this sea of confusion and inequality is the midwife. She can show women ways to avoid the pitfalls of the system while guiding her towards a safe outcome. As an advocate, the midwife is well placed to have a beneficial impact not only on the woman and her birth, but on the very system itself. There are many strengths that a midwife brings to this advocacy role:

- She knows the hospital intimately.
- She knows the personnel who work there, their preferences, methods and foibles.
- She know the routines and protocols, how these were established and the mechanism for changing them.
- As a professional equal of the doctor, she has a right to challenge and question his practises, if she feels they are detrimental or questionable.
- She has a good understanding of normal birth and can recognise complications, should they occur.
- She has a vested interest in keeping the pregnancy and labour normal, since it enhances her own professional skills.
- She knows where to get the evidence to back her assertions, and where to seek support for her views.
- She has more time for women, and is often willing to go the extra mile on their behalf.
- She is usually a woman herself, which gives her insights that are difficult (if not impossible) for men to obtain or even understand because of their inherent biological differences in the area of instinctive reproductive behaviours.

It is unfair to expect pregnant women to take responsibility for changing the health care system. Midwives themselves often complain of having little enough influence and that they find it difficult to improve services. If midwives are finding it hard, given that they know the people involved and are ideally placed to exert some pressure, how can consumers be expected to shoulder the burden of turning around a system which they find a total mystery? Sometimes, the father of the baby is expected to assume the advocacy role and speak up on his partner's behalf. Yet, he too, is totally unfamiliar with the ways of hospitals and has the additional handicap of being torn between wanting to support his partner's wishes, while attempting to appease the staff. Many expectant parents are steamrollered into accepting care that is convenient for the hospital or its staff because they are unable to fight the system. That parents should need to even consider fighting for their rights is an indictment of maternity care as it is organised now, and it will take much goodwill and effort to convince parents that their needs and wishes will automatically be respected without question and the services they request will be cheerfully provided. Whilst birth continues to be centred in hospitals, the battles will go on, because there will always be conflict between the medical model of care enshrined in the hospital setting and the social nature of a process more fittingly rooted in the community.

Informed choice

The basic principle of a woman's right to know all the risks and benefits of proposed treatments is accepted as the foundation of equitable and effective maternity care. Putting these principles into practice is often problematic. A number of factors influence a woman's ability to exercise her right to make informed choices:

- She may not have access to accurate and scientifically valid information.
- The information she is offered may be inadvertently (or even deliberately) limited or censored by the person giving it, as a reflection of personal bias or in an attempt to encourage her to choose an option favoured by others.
- The information may not have been presented in a way that she can readily understand.
- Her state of physical or emotional health may reduce her ability to think clearly, evaluate her options or make a decision.
- She may feel pressured or coerced into making snap decisions, if she is not given time for due consideration.
- She may lack support for her chosen plan of action.
- She may not be given the right to change her mind later, is she wishes.

There are basic concepts inherent in a truly informed choice, and these are outlined below.

The concept of an informed choice

An informed choice is one in which:

◆ Accurate information, based on the current scientific evidence, is provided in a sensitive and non-threatening manner,

◆ Specific choice points are described in detail,

◆ The advantages and disadvantages (risks) are clearly explained,

◆ Evaluation is made to ensure that the information is understood,

◆ Enough time is given for consideration of the physical, psychological and emotional implication of each choice,

◆ Crisis decisions, based on information which is unavailable to the parents, are delegated to the medical attendants.

◆ Emotional support is available, regardless of the decision made.

Exercising the right to informed choice

In addition, there are a number of discrete steps involved in the making of a decision. Most adults are very familiar with this process, since taking responsibility for one's own actions is a hallmark of maturity. Many times we speed through these steps almost unconsciously and have no trouble negotiating the various stages. When major life decisions are required, we usually take more time, and work out way deliberately through each phase, since we know that snap decisions, especially with important issues, can lead to later regrets. Many of the situations faced by women during their pregnancies and labours fall into this category: they are making decisions that affect not only themselves, but their babies, at a time when they may not feel well equipped, for the reasons listed above, to take this responsibility.

Since the need to make decisions arises as a result of a problem that requires a solution, the broad task is really that of problem solving. The steps in this process are:

1. Identifying the problem requiring resolution. Deciding if the problem is one you should deal with, rather than someone else.

2. Determining the desired outcome. In other words, what is your goal in solving this problem — what are you hoping to achieve?

3. What possible solutions can be considered? There are many ways to solve a problem, and during this stage it is useful to list as many as possible, even if some seem fanciful or impractical. A extensive list of potential solutions encourages lateral thinking.

4. Analysis of each solution in turn. This means evaluating each one against a set of personal criteria, such as: how you feel about it; what risks (for

yourself and others) might be inherent in this option; whether it is within your power to achieve; whether it reflects your values and philosophy. Careful analysis enables each option to be weighed carefully in the light of these factors.

5. Choosing a solution.

6. Acting upon it.

7. Evaluating the eventual outcomes. Did you achieve your goal, or do you need to return to step three and try another solution?

Women are often asked to exercise their right of choice without being offered assistance in working through these steps. For some, the whole process of problem solving may be unfamiliar, as a result of a lifetime of relationships where other people have made the decisions on their behalf. Others will be accustomed to working through problem solving in this way, perhaps because they are older (and have more general life experience) or have worked in jobs involving the management of people or tasks to some degree. Avoid making assumptions about womens' capabilities in this area of problem solving. Many women will be comfortable with the idea of exercising choice, while for others, the making of any decision will be a triumph (regardless of what the decision actually is). Midwives can assist women with these steps in problem solving, either by identifying the various steps in the process, or by providing information about alternative options that could be considered. Supporting the final decision is also important, as is later evaluation and reflection (as part of debriefing).

Opportunities for advocacy during pregnancy

How can midwives advocate for parents during the pregnancy? Let us examine some possibilities.

➡ Have contact with women as early as possible in their pregnancy. There are many ways of advertising your services to make sure that women can locate you, and some of these are listed in Chapter 9.

➡ Provide information about the health care system itself, the way the services are organised and the mechanisms for using it. By doing this, you will be fully informing women of their options for pregnancy care.

➡ Discuss the various medical tests and fetal surveillance methods they will be offered. Parents need the facts about these tests — the disadvantages and alternatives as well as their benefits. Avoid assuming that parents will view pre-natal testing in a similar way to yourself. Risk assessment should be undertaken by those having the tests, and your views may differ markedly from theirs. For example, a one-in-one-hundred risk may seem high to you, but low to a pregnant woman, when she weighs it up.

➡ If she has language problems or sensitive cultural needs, make arrangements for interpreters or appropriate companions for pre-natal visits, tests etc. All women have a right to information, even if they cannot speak the predominant language. It is your responsibility to provide the necessary assistance so she is able to participate fully in her care.

➡ If she requests your help, speak on her behalf during negotiations about social problems. Her health, and that of the baby, may depend on finding ways of improving her social situation, and you may have the necessary contacts or be able to deal with the authorities central to solving her problems. There may even be occasions when you need to act without her consent, especially if you suspect that her life is in danger.

➡ Talk to her family, and her partner if this will improve communication or enable better social support to be obtained. Once again, you should seek her permission before attempting this course of action, and be clear about what she wants you to say or do. Acting as an advocate for her within her family can be tricky, but sometimes an "authority" figure can impose reason and promote discussion that otherwise may not take place.

➡ Convene case meetings with other team members if this will promote better communication and more co-ordinated care. You may have more insight into her needs than other team members who may not have had the same amount of contact with her. If you are the lead professional then co-ordination will automatically be your role; if others are primary care givers, then your advocacy on her behalf may be especially important.

During labour and birth

There are times during labour when women really can't speak for themselves. The intensity of the contractions, the need to concentrate fully, the impact of endorphins on thought processes all mitigate against a woman being able to think clearly and rationally. This is often seen as a "weakness", and is sometimes used as a reason for others to take over or as an excuse for limiting her involvement in the making of decisions.

Conversely, and problematically, the current trend for insisting that women participate fully can conflict with her need to fully immerse herself in her labour, which is impossible if there are distractions. As long as labour is progressing normally, then there should be no need for her to engage in the intellectual activity involved in exercising choice — everyone will be following her lead and her body will be doing its job well. If a woman's body senses danger during labour or she is disturbed, it will be difficult for her to react spontaneously in the free and uninhibited way associated with instinctive behaviour. The subtle and insidious pressure imposed by the setting and its personnel can require her to maintain a degree of alertness at all times, in case she needs to take protective action. It is similar to making love with one eye on the door in case anyone comes in! This is where the midwife, acting as an advocate, can provide a buffer between the woman in labour and the outside world.

If a complication does arise or a threat appears in some form, her natural reaction will be one of self preservation, and her focus will automatically shift from her internal state to her external circumstances. This is the normal, and desired, effect of adrenalin. She will then be able to interact with others, as her head clears (from the fall in her endorphin levels) and her alert state enables her to take appropriate action. She can then act as her own advocate, in her own best interests.

Some practical measures that can be used by a midwife advocating for a woman's needs in labour are described in Chapter 6. In addition to these ideas, specific events or situations may arise that require considered action by the midwife. Some examples are described below.

⇒ In the area of maternity care, women are often confused by the myriad of new experiences and the apparent complexity of the whole event. They may have very limited information from which to formulate solutions to problems, and this can lead to dependent behaviour and over reliance on caregivers. One of your primary tasks will be to answer her questions and explain the options for her care, and she will appreciate your taking this interest in her (one of the most valued aspects of midwifery care mentioned by women). In giving her the details she seeks, remember the elements of good communication mentioned in Chapter 3. Some of the suggestions for enhancing learning described in Chapter 9 are also appropriate in this situation.

⇒ Make sure that she is not subjected to unnecessary intervention during labour. There are many "routines" that are applied to women gratuitously with no regard for their specific needs, just because the procedure has been listed in the standing orders. Carrying these out, without due consideration and the obtaining of full consent from the woman, is not only a gross act of betrayal by a midwife, but one which could also have legal ramifications (see below). Protocols should be regarded as guidelines, not as strict orders. At all times, you must be able to justify (defend) your reasons for intervening, and these should be noted in the woman's records. Your knowledge of the physiology of normal labour and its many variations will prove useful in describing what is happening and explaining your actions.

If doctors are insisting that you follow their generalised instructions for their clients, you have no obligation to undertake procedures that you feel, in your professional opinion, are unwise or unsafe. This is particularly true for private patients, and you may better protect the woman (and yourself) by requesting that the doctor himself attend to his patient.

Another way of managing this issue is to have the protocols changed. There will be a mechanism for evaluating and establishing protocols, and you need to find out how this works. Ways of doing this are included in Chapter 10.

An accessible source of instant reference, such as the Cochrane Library, could be invaluable in establishing evidence based practice with the maternity unit. This database can be installed on the hospital's computer system for easy access by all staff. Other ways of ensuring that standards are established using the best evidence available include establishing a professional lending library, circulating key articles circulated amongst staff and regular in-service training are. A climate of healthy enquiry and a recognition of the importance of on-going learning flows from open-minded and progressive unit managers. In the past, innovation and peer review have been lacking in maternity units, and the recent development of performance-based contracts may help to bring this area of the health services into line with other branches.

➡ Respect her wishes for giving birth. This sounds elementary, yet is can be difficult to achieve in practice. The protocols and personal preferences of caregivers often take precedence over a woman's desires in labour, especially if her requests are seen to be unusual. You can protect her rights more easily if you know what she has in mind. Written birth plans, often discussed and compiled during the pre-natal consultations or classes, give an indication of her wishes. This written record should be broad in its scope and not too prescriptive, to allow for flexibility according to the circumstances. If she has no formal written document, you can easily record any special requests in her notes when you are completing the initial paperwork during her admission into the labour ward. Some simple questions will trigger the important points:

"What would you specially like us to do for you?"

"Have you prepared to labour in any particular way?"

"Who would you like to have with you during labour, and at the birth?"

"Have you given any thought to how you would like to give birth?"

"Is there anything you would like us to know about you, so we can help you more easily?"

When you record her answers in the notes, put the statements in her words: "(Name) says she would like ... during labour" etc. This is a powerful way of indicating those approaches for which you have consent, as distinct from those for which you have no mandate. This is very useful tool for the midwife advocate, who can clearly say that she is carrying out the stated wishes of the woman (while making it clear that there is no consent for other approaches).

When working with women during labour, and particularly it you are advocating on their behalf, it is vital that you avoid making assumptions about what women want. Many times you may think you know a woman well enough to guess how she will view aspects of her care, and will be surprised when she chooses so do something quite different. Women can be fickle, and the stresses of labour can make women think completely differently!

To avoid confusion, and perhaps later recrimination, try to establish a clear indication of what she desires, preferably before labour or in the early stages. Straight questions and honest answers are valuable is avoiding supposition and assumptions. The only time when you need to tread cautiously in fulfilling her stated requests is when she is passing through the transitional phase of labour: her natural tendency for irrational thinking and confusion at that time needs to be recognised as symptoms of progress rather than as lucid instructions to be followed.

➡ Offer her access to her medical records, especially while she is still in the hospital. The information they contain could be essential is enabling her to accept the outcome of the birth and in helping her to understand why certain procedures were done. Gaining access to records after she leaves hospital is not always simple, yet is it possible, and you should become familiar with the process involved so you can advise her how to do it.

➡ If she is unhappy with her care, you can suggest ways she can register her complaints. Writing to the hospital (the maternity unit manager, the hospital administration or the board, as appropriate) places her concern on record and may trigger an investigation, that not only provides her with useful answers, but highlights areas of care that could be improved for all women. Encouraging her to talk to the staff involved at the birth is another way of establishing dialogue that may resolve worrying issues.

Honest, open discussion, especially after a disastrous outcome, may head off a later lawsuit, which some women will feel obliged to initiate in order to get sought after answers. Some countries have formal mechanisms available, usually through a statutory body, for patients to lodge complaints about health care services. Being familiar with these services, and how they can be used, is an important part of your role as a midwife. Using the media is another way of highlighting inadequacies in care, and may be a last resort if other avenues have proven unsuccessful.

➡ Advocating for your colleagues is an indirect way of supporting women, and one that could be recognised as central to improving birth outcomes. Midwives seem notoriously poor at supporting and protecting each other, particularly over practise issues. Pregnant women need to know that their carers have a collective philosophy, and consistency in their approach. When midwives cannot work together as a team by pooling their resources to provide a strong force for change, it will be the women who will ultimately suffer from fragmented care, disharmony and demoralisation amongst disgruntled staff. These emotions inevitably flow on to other relationships, and a woman who is struggling to find her own way through a confusing health care system needs strong role models and a confident, "can-do" attitude from her carers. There are further ideas on how midwives can achieve these goals in the final chapter.

What about the legalities?

This is a complex question, involving ethical dilemmas, the law and standards of practice. There is not scope in this book to canvass these issues thoroughly, and other texts, specifically geared to these issues are recommended (Dimond 1994; Jenkins 1995). A brief summary of the major points and issues is discussed here, with the aim of laying a foundation on which specific strategies for advocacy can be laid.

A midwife is always responsible for her own professional practice, regardless of the setting in which she works. It is incumbent on you to ensure that you are providing the best care possible and exercising your judgement wisely within the framework of your employment contract, the common law and your professional code of practice. The increasing awareness in the community of consumer's rights and the law generally has stepped up the pressure on all health professionals, and practices that were likely to go unnoticed in the past are now being subjected to close scrutiny. In this increasingly litigious society, midwives can be regarded as at low risk of being sued for several reasons:

• They are dealing primarily with normal, health women, undergoing an innately safe, normal physiological process.

• Any women with complications are referred to specialist doctors for treatment. Thus midwives should not be called upon to perform treatments beyond their skills or to act in ways for which they are untrained. Of course, sometimes an emergency will require a midwife to act on her own initiative, without medical assistance, and she needs to take steps to protect herself in these circumstances.

- Midwives generally spend more time with women during the pregnancy and labour and have a greater opportunity to develop a positive working relationships with them.

- Midwives usually have good communication skills and are comfortable in discussing emotional and psychological issues with women in their care. This can be very important in establishing rapport, and is particularly valuable in debriefing sessions following the birth.

- Midwives have good access to the increasing body of scientific evidence supporting their practice.

- Midwives are (generally) women, and while this may not save a midwife from a charge of poor practice (and nor should it), the capacity for a midwife to really tune in to women, the result of common instincts, provides a strong link between herself and the pregnant woman. Natural insight and empathy can be gained from the common bonds that women share.

As midwives extend their roles and practices to encompass a variety of workplace settings and tasks, their exposure to the legal ramifications of their work will also increase. A midwife working in an independent practice carries additional responsibility over one employed by a hospital; a midwife performing peripheral tasks, such as prescribing contraceptives, undertaking lactation counselling or advising on other women's health issues is more vulnerable if she is undertaking additional treatments not strictly within her remit, unless she has undergone additional training.

Legal issues fall into two general areas: those involving malpractice and those involving assault. Success in a malpractice suit depends on the claimant being able to prove that the care carried out was negligent. Assault cases revolve around the issue of informed consent, and whether permission was given by the patient for the treatment to be carried out. In both cases, demonstrable harm to either the mother or baby must be shown to have occurred.

Since midwives are required to refer any complicated cases to medical colleagues, there should be few opportunities for parents to claim that a midwife acted negligently. However, since everyone makes mistakes, and clinical issues are not always clear cut, occasionally a midwife will find herself being sued for malpractice. It is for this reason that midwives in independent practice must carry professional indemnity insurance, for the protection of themselves and the parents. Midwives working for a hospital are covered by their employer's insurance.

It is also unlikely that a midwife will be sued for assault, since she is generally scrupulously careful to make sure that she has permission from the woman for any treatment she carries out, and for any action that she needs to take. Misunderstandings can occur and communication can break down, especially

141

in situations of crisis, when immediate action may be necessary. Usually parents will accept the need for intervention when the life of their baby is at risk, but if it later proves that the concern was unfounded, then some women may feel justified in challenging the actions taken.

Legal systems vary from country to country (the law works differently in the United States, both in content and practice from that operating in Great Britain and Australia, for instance) and also compensation arrangements for parents differ. Private health insurance, public health care systems and professional indemnity arrangements all affect the legal climate in which a woman is giving birth. The influence of litigation on Australian medical practice was recently exposed in a wide ranging Government Report, released in 1995 (Tito 1995). In general, there are some basic principles that apply in all jurisdictions:

- No practitioner can undertake any treatment without receiving the expressed consent of the patient, and this consent must be fully informed and given willingly. The definition of a treatment includes a range of procedures, from the simple, such as taking someone's blood pressure, to the complex, such as undertaking a caesarean section. Debate about what constitutes "fully informed" consent was settled in Australia (which has implications for cases brought under British law) in 1991 when the High Court of Australia (Rogers vs Whittaker) ruled that a patient must be told all the side effects of a treatment, not just those considered significant by the caregiver. Until this decision was handed down, doctors had been able to exercise their judgement in deciding how much a patient needed to be told, and this frequently led to patients receiving "filtered" information on which to base their decisions. Now, patients are being given much more detail about proposed treatment as doctors work to reduce their risk of being sued for not obtaining fully informed consent.

  Later cases have confirmed the High Court's view that since the patient is the one undergoing the treatment, only they can assess the degree of risk involved and evaluate it in light of their personal circumstances. The days when doctors accidentally or deliberately skewing the information given to patients are over, and this is an outcome with implications for midwifery, as we shall see below.

- Whatever the patient decides to do must be respected by the caregivers, even when the chosen course of action would seem to be unwise (parents, too, will make mistakes and have outcomes that were unexpected). This right can be difficult to maintain and protect when the unborn baby would appear to be at risk from a parental decision. Again, the law in the United Kingdom and Australia says that the unborn baby has no legal rights that must be considered ahead of its mother. The situation in the

United States is less clear, and the celebrated cases of women being sued for the abuse of a child in utero (and similar actions) are becoming less frequent as the ramifications of this approach are more closely evaluated.

Women have an intense desire to do the best for their babies, a fact that has sometimes been used in the past to gain their compliance in the application of unnecessary or inappropriate treatments. They may not always know the best way to achieve this outcome and may not always be in a position to give their unborn baby the best care (due to her social circumstances, for example), but their fierce protection of the baby must be accepted and supported, even if it makes caregivers uncomfortable. It is easy to judge others and proffer advice, and much harder to stand beside a woman in her struggle to do her best, particularly when the outcome was not as she hoped. This is a special challenge for the midwife.

If a woman, having listened to your professional advice, decides on a course of action which you feel is unsafe or professionally unacceptable, what do you do then? In the United Kingdom, a midwife is legally required to remain with the woman and provide care to the best of her ability. The midwife must inform her supervisors of the situation, and summon extra help if that is appropriate. She will not be prosecuted if the birth goes badly as a result of the parent's decision, but her practice may be scrutinised to ensure that everything was done as required by law.

In other countries where this kind of protective legislation does not exist, midwives may face legal problems in supporting women's choices. There are many examples of midwives being censured or even deregistered for assisting women at births where parental decisions led to disaster. It is difficult for a midwife to leave a woman who needs her skills, and it can be argued that the midwife has a professional duty of care to assist. Common decency would also suggest that to walk away from a potential disaster in order to save one's own professional standing is unacceptable in a caring community. Until the appropriate legislation is in place (such as that covering doctors who are required in emergency situations to offer what treatment they can), midwives will find themselves in untenable circumstances from time to time.

This is especially likely in the case of homebirths, where, as the only professional in attendance, the midwife can be challenged more readily about her actions. If the climate in the community is hostile or wary of homebirth, the scene may be set for the kind of "witch hunt" described by Marsden Wagner (1995). Regulation of home birth practice not only offers protection for consumers, but is undeniable proof of community acceptance of home birth as a woman's right. Well written regulations are also protective of midwives, giving them a framework in which to practice, legal protection, and recognition of their qualifications and experience.

143

Reducing your legal vulnerability

Although very few midwives have been sued, as midwifery moves more into the realms of independent practice the potential for legal challenge will automatically grow. While this is a frightening prospect for many aspiring independent practitioners, it can be seen as a measure of the responsibility and standing. There are a number of steps you can take to minimise your exposure and risk of litigation, including:

➡ Take out appropriate professional indemnity insurance. It may be expensive, but it is a necessary pre-requisite for independent practice.

➡ Carefully screen your clients, and encourage parents to choose an appropriate birth place according to their needs: high risk women may do better with midwifery care, but in a hospital setting with back up facilities, rather than at home. If the midwife has established a good working relationship with the hospital, and has visiting rights, there should be no impediment for her attending the woman in that setting, and reducing the risk of a poor outcome due to a lack of necessary equipment and personnel if there is a problem in the home.

➡ Document your care as fully as possible. Comprehensive notes are essential to demonstrate that the care offered was professional and at an acceptable standard.

➡ Make sure that your practice is evidence based and in line with current scientific thinking. As more is discovered about the risks, benefits and effects of treatments, your treatment methods may need to change. Keep up to date with you reading and have regular discussions with colleagues, to hone your skills and update your knowledge base.

➡ Know where to obtain extra resources when required. This could include assistance from a colleague, specialised equipment, medical back up, written information and sources of support.

➡ Communicate with the parents, and involve them in solving problems that affect their care. Honesty and a straightforward approach are essential to avoid confusion and misunderstanding. Parents will need answers when disasters occur, and in extreme circumstances, may use the courts to obtain information they feel has been withheld. Admitting that mistakes have been made is an important strategy in avoiding the creation of an impression that professional carers are covering up facts in an attempt to protect themselves. Poor practice needs to be exposed, so the caregiver can learn from mistakes and to ensure justice for the parents. Honest mistakes by a caregiver may be accepted by grieving parents whereas attempts to hide important errors may fuel a natural desire to pinpoint blame and extract revenge.

➡ Know your limitations. As a midwife, you understand the wide range of behaviours associated with normal birth, and the danger signs of impending complications. Accept your level of skills and training and know when to refer the woman to others better qualified to help. The women in your care are relying on you to practice midwifery, not medicine, and they expect that you will arrange for onward referral if there is any problem that requires specialised care. They may not accept your actions at a later date if they feel a better outcome could have been obtained if timely transfer or referral had been made.

➡ Arrange for regular debriefing with a senior colleague as a means of self-assessment and learning. It is important to talk problems through, and to incorporate reflective evaluation of your care into your practice. Every midwife has something to learn, since women giving birth offer so many possible outcomes, and regular discussions with senior colleagues or those is associated fields (such as medicine) will strengthen your practice and confidence. When a disaster occurs it is imperative to have a mechanism in place to deal with your own feelings and reactions to that they can be resolved. Without this help, there is a risk that your emotions may colour your management of future pregnancies, perhaps with detrimental effects on yourself and your clients.

Direct action as an advocate

The practical application of advocacy skills is a challenge for most midwives. You will find it easier to speak for women if you learn basic negotiation skills and ways of resolving conflict. These are best refined through participation in interactive workshops, and there are suitable courses available through many adult education facilities. Such courses need not be geared specifically for midwives as the skills are generic to many life situations. There are also a number of books available that offer step by step programs for learning the skills of assertiveness and negotiation, and a selection of these are listed in the appendix.

When the times comes to act, some simple strategies may prove useful:

➡ Try to anticipate potential sources of conflict and take steps in advance to defuse the situation. An argument can sometimes be thwarted if you take the initiative: you know what the hospital protocols are; you are aware of the personal foibles of other members of staff; and the practice methods of your peers and colleagues are familiar to you. You could have a discussion with the doctor concerned before you try something new with his patient (such as supporting her request for no third stage oxytocics). You could offer to take the place of a midwife unwilling to experiment with an unfamiliar technique requested by the parents (such as performing an internal examination with the woman standing). You could provide written information for your colleagues to read so that they have some background knowledge of new management techniques (for example, quelling some fears by reading about water birth before they see it in practice).

➥ Avoid arguing with colleagues in front of the labouring woman and her partner. If, for example, you know that her chosen course of action is likely to antagonise the doctor when he arrives, prepare him for what has been requested before he arrives on the scene. A possible conversation is described below.

Try not to pitch an unsuspecting colleague into an unfamiliar situation without warning, especially if their unpreparedness is likely to cause them professional embarrassment. Show that you are willing to be supportive and to assist, by discussing the situation in advance and away from the client. The example given describes one way this can be done.

A conversation with a caregiver in second stage

Midwife (on the phone): "Hello doctor. (Name) has started pushing, and is now in second stage, so it is time for you to come. When you get here, you will see that she has chosen to kneel on the floor on a mat, and is leaning over her partner. I know that this is unusual, but I have checked in her notes and it says there that she said she wanted to choose her own position in second stage. When I asked her, she said that she was comfortable and couldn't possible move. I realise that this may be a little awkward for us, so I have found a low stool for you to sit on and placed the things you will need within reach. She seems to be very happy and doing well. So, we will see you soon?"

A short time later, the doctor comes into the room. The midwife is kneeling down beside the woman, who is grunting and pushing from time to time.

Midwife (over her shoulder): "Oh, hello Dr (Name). Things are going really well here. (Name) is pushing very effectively, and the baby seems to be coming quite quickly. The stool is there for you to sit on, and your gloves and your other things are on that sterile sheet beside her. It won't be long now!"

Later, after the birth, in the nurses station:

Midwife: "You know that was really terrific. I was surprised how easily the baby was born. I guess it was the extra gravity that made the difference, and the fact she could open her pelvis wide when she was kneeling like that. She was very grateful for your assistance, and asked me pass on her special thanks. I really felt quite uncomfortable — this was the first time I had caught a baby like this, and I just wanted to thank you too for your support."

➡ Make sure you have recorded the woman's wishes in her notes. This makes it clear that:

this is the mother's idea,

she has given her consent for this approach,

she has not given her consent for any alternatives,

it is not your idea — you are not pushing your agenda, and

there is little choice but to make the best of it.

➡ Coercion of the woman can be avoided if she is unable to make eye-contact with those demanding her submission. She will automatically close her eyes if her head is resting on something (perhaps by facing her partner and holding on around his neck), and this also makes it less likely that she will open her eyes to pay attention to the request/demand. In addition, if her back is to the door and to the caregivers, her privacy and concentration are more likely to be maintained.

➡ Try to keep her off the bed. As soon as she settles onto a bed she is more likely to take on the role of a patient: passive, submissive and vulnerable. With her feet on a floormat she will be upright, autonomous and more able to take charge. Caregivers unused to being with women who are not reclining on a bed will be momentarily thrown off guard, and they will be forced to try the new approach, habits and routines being abandoned in the process. The resultant birth will be unique, challenging and exciting for the parents and remembered by everyone.

➡ Make sure that you are performing midwifery care not medical tasks. Leave the episiotomy, the routine timing of stages, the affixing of fetal heart monitors, the rupturing of membranes etc. to the doctors. You could force them to evaluate their interventions by asking the question "Is this really necessary?". Simple statements such as "The tissues are really stretching very easily", "the labour is slow but there are signs of progress" and "gravity will help bring the baby down more quickly" may force the reassessment of a routine intervention.

➡ Try to confront issues rather than deal with them in passively aggressive ways. For example, instead of hiding the episiotomy scissors, or dropping the forceps (common "tricks" used by midwives to forestall intervention) a quiet discussion with the doctor, away from his patients, shows your concern and avoids arguments in front of the woman. In addition, if a midwife routinely calls the doctor very late in second stage in an effort to avoid his use of lift-out forceps (for example) then he may become suspicious of her skills in assessing progress and this could undermine his respect for midwifery. A more honest approach would be to politely and professionally challenge his approach, using the same assertiveness skills expected of parents. In questioning a colleague, chal-

147

lenge the issue not the person. Instead of saying "why are you doing a forceps on this woman?" try saying "Why is it necessary for forceps to be used here?". By doing this you will avoid a personal attack that could undermine valuable trust.

➡ Stay with the woman in a physical way. Align yourself with her body posture, and at her level. With your eyes on her, it will be harder for you to be coerced into manoeuvring her into some other position that she does not want to adopt.

➡ Remind her that she will need to give you permission to act on her behalf and that you may need support for taking this role if the situation demands it. She may have asked you to write her wishes in her records for later reference, but when the time comes and you say "(Name) said earlier that she wanted to have her baby this way" or "(Name) has asked us not to perform an episiotomy" she may need to reinforce your position by saying something like "That's right" or "It's in the notes". The father may be able to help here if the woman is unable to speak due to her concentration on the contractions.

➡ After the birth is over, positive feedback to those colleagues to stepped outside their normal routine to try something new will encourage them to try it again. Acknowledgment and appreciation go a long way to supporting change in personal practice and are more effective than carping criticism. People like to be thanked for special efforts and if this feedback also comes from the woman and her partner, it is doubly worthwhile.

Acting as an advocate is a new and challenging role for many midwives, and is an essential component in achieving change in hospital practices and improving birth outcomes for women and babies. Women can only become empowered if their caregivers enable them to take power and to exercise their right of choice in a supportive environment. Midwives who feel strong and capable are better able to support and empower the women in their care. Learning how to act as an advocate will not only strengthen your professional standing, but enable women to take their rightful place at the centre of the maternity health care system.

References

Dimond B. 1994, *The Legal Aspects of Midwifery*, Books for Midwives Press, UK.

Jenkins R. 1995, *The Law and the Midwife*, Blackwell Science, UK.

Tito F. 1995, *Compensation and Professional Indemnity in Health Care*, Commonwealth Department of Human Services and Health, Canberra.

Wagner M. 1995, 'A global witch-hunt', *Lancet*, vol. 346, pp. 1020–22.

Chapter 9

THE POTENTIAL OF PRE-NATAL EDUCATION

Women who are expecting their first baby are possibly more open to learning at this time than at any other in their adult lives. The whole adventure of being pregnant, the mystery of the baby growing inside, the intensity of new emotions and the wonderment of it all combine to arouse intense curiosity. There are so many questions to ask, so many new experiences to assimilate, so many preparations to make that it can seem as though the learning will never end (and it could be argued that indeed the pregnancy and birth are just the beginning).

Working with women during this time, especially as a guide and mentor, is enormously rewarding for a midwife. The role is not one of direction or advising, but rather of a supportive presence. It is similar to standing by as a child takes its first tentative steps: instruction or advice have no impact; all one can do is be ready to catch if there is a fall or be there to lean on if the effort is too much. Only the child can take the steps, all we can do is watch with amazement and excitement as these first efforts towards independence are attempted.

The special relationship a woman has with her midwife places you in a key position. By being available to answer questions, provide her with information and other resources and listen as she explores her feelings, you can help her grow into the responsibilities of parenthood. Each time she comes to you for help, you can enable her to develop the skills she will need to nurture her baby and blossom as a woman and mother. The unique opportunity presented by your professional relationship can be embraced and used in a way that empowers you both, on an equal footing, as one woman to another.

The system of maternity care in most westernised countries has been designed, at times seemingly deliberately, to reduce the potential of this powerful outcome. Midwifery care has been fragmented, with midwives often unable to act as primary caregivers for a woman's entire pregnancy and birth. Instead, the pregnant woman sees a procession of different midwives, all with different approaches, all unable to form the holistic view of her as a person that comes automatically with continuity of carer. Conflicting advice, pinpointed by women as a major complaint of the post-partum period, in fact begins during the pregnancy, as many different health professionals offer their own ideas and prescriptions. In addition, this approach hampers midwives in their efforts to gain confidence and understanding from seeing the pregnancy and birth through to its conclusion in the early post-partum period.

On the other side of the equation are the women — a whole variety, each with her own needs, feelings, attitudes and values. Whilst all women may have their baby's health and well-being as a foremost goal, some believe that these outcomes are most likely to be achieved in a high-tech hospital, with all the gadgetry and medical paraphernalia that can be applied. Central to their vision of a good birth may be feeling no pain ("why suffer?"), obtained via an epidural to numb and distance the powerful sensations of giving birth. These women need good nursing care — they don't need a midwife to supervise all the technology and implement the medical regimes.

Women who think like this, whilst no less deserving of good care and empathy, can be a disappointment for a midwife. Being with this woman in labour relegates the midwife to being a specialised nurse. Professional satisfaction can be achieved from assisting a woman with medicalised birth, but there is nothing like the thrill and excitement of a spontaneous physiological birth, particularly when it occurs in a hospital setting — a normal physiological birth can be such a rarity that it is talked about for weeks!

There are women for whom pregnancy and birth are exciting challenges within the normal life cycle and for whom birth holds no terrors. For them, birth is a normal life passage, perhaps full of mystery and potential, with its own rewards for the hard work involved. These women are pure joy for a midwife, as they offer a chance to witness the raw power of nature at the same time as fulfilling her full professional role. Sometimes, though, it seems as if these women are disappearing, as more succumb to the pressures to conform imposed by western systems of medicalised maternity care.

How can we motivate and inspire women to embrace natural birth as an achievable and worthwhile goal? Better education for women pre-natally may hold the key. If we can work with women at a time when they are hungry for information and ready to soak up the details like a sponge, we must be able to make some impact. It may be difficult, with deeply rooted cultural beliefs to overcome, intense personal feelings to be explored and entrenched negative attitudes to turn around, yet we must take every opportunity we have to reach out to women, and the pre-natal period is an ideal time.

In a perfect maternity system, each pregnant woman would have her own personal midwife, who gets to know her, works with her, supports, comforts and educates her through the months of pregnancy before accompanying her through the birth itself. In practice, however, these ideal systems are still rare overall. It is more likely that the midwife will see many women only briefly, without the opportunity to really work with them in an on-going way. The moves towards caseload practice will improve this situation for many women and midwives, but until this approach is universally adopted, others ways of improving the service must be found. Even in less than perfect circumstances, there are still opportunities for educating women during their pregnancies, and every chance must be grasped.

As a midwife, you will come into contact with pregnant women in a variety of settings, such as:

- during supervision of labour ward tours
- in pre-natal clinics
- when supervising pre-natal testing, such as CTGs or ultrasounds
- when booking women into the hospital
- during a pre-natal admission to hospital e.g. for treatment of high blood pressure, or fetal assessment
- in post-natal wards, when they visit friends
- over the phone, when they call for information
- in social settings, perhaps through family or friends
- in the community, and
- in pre-natal classes.

Every one of these occasions presents an opportunity for valuable pre-natal education. To make the most of the interaction, it helps to have a clear idea of the overall goals you have for the woman in question, that is, what you hope she derives from her contact with you. You can use these conversations to:

- inform her
- empower her
- promote her personal growth
- enhance her problem solving skills

- increase her self awareness
- build her self-esteem and confidence, and
- enable her to take responsibility

apart from answering her questions, which of course you will do! Apart from just giving information, achieving these outcomes will be made easier by the adoption of a number of strategies, such as:

➡ Avoiding giving advice. Instead, ask her what solutions she has already thought of to solve her problem, and offer other suggestions for her to consider, as appropriate.

➡ Offering broad solutions from a holistic viewpoint. Many apparently medical problems have their basis in poor social conditions, which may need addressing first.

➡ Basing your information on treatment options on the scientific evidence for their efficacy and safety.

➡ Inviting her to decide on the solution that seems most likely to fit her needs, as she sees them.

➡ Explaining options in clear, jargon-free language. If necessary, provide pictures, diagrams, or demonstrations to clarify anything she doesn't understand.

➡ Listening attentively as she speaks, and acknowledging, validating and confirming what you have heard.

➡ Making no assumptions about who she is, what she knows, or how she feels.

➡ Supporting her decisions, whatever they are.

➡ Offering her a chance to reflect on and evaluate the decision she has made and the chance to change her mind.

Learning how to educate others requires specialised training not usually included in basic midwifery courses. Discovering ways of incorporating the basic principles of adult learning into every educational opportunity is stimulating and rewarding. It is also a process beyond the scope of this book. There are a number of resources available that focus on the needs of adult learners within the broad setting of maternity care and these are listed in the appendix.

Some of the broader issues, especially where they relate to midwives and their individual encounters with women are described here.

Giving information

Have you ever been in a situation where you thought that you had told a woman what she needed to know and answered her questions satisfactorily only to discover later that she seemed to have completely misunderstood what you said? This is a common scenario, and one that can be very frustrating for the well-intentioned midwife. Often the woman is blamed for her lack of understanding (because of her lack of education, or inability to speak the language for example), as this seems to be the answer to the problem. However, the responsibility for good communication in a midwife/woman relationship usually rests with the midwife, particularly if questions are being asked and information is being sought by the pregnant mother. If you are not getting through to her, then you will have to explore some new approaches to avoid further confusion and embarrassment. There are a number of steps you can take.

➡ Check her background before you start the conversation. If she speaks little English, then find an interpreter, or written materials in her own language (provided she can read her own language). If you have some idea of where she lives, her educational level and family situation, you will be in a better position to tailor your language to her level of understanding. This does not mean "talking down" to her, just re-phrasing technical terms and unfamiliar concepts into straightforward, every-day language she uses herself.

➡ Have a number of teaching resources available to use if necessary. If she doesn't understand your verbal instructions, for example, having a series of diagrams or a model to illustrate your message might help. Showing her appropriate pieces of equipment — a speculum, fetal scalp electrode clip, amnihook, cord clamp etc. (be careful not to frighten her) may increase her understanding. Be aware that sometimes the visual impact of equipment, drawings and especially videos can create anxiety where none existed before. If this happens, take time to debrief and examine the reasons for her fears.

➡ Talking to another woman who has had a similar experience is an excellent way of providing information and addressing associated feelings. Support groups are a marvellous way of building networks, and sharing common experiences with others is an important social process. Look for ways of bringing women together — arranging the seats in the pre-natal clinic in clusters facing each other is a simple measure that encourages conversations in small groups. Teaming up a woman with particular needs with a buddy can be useful. This is a culturally appropriate way to approach education for many people, and setting up this kind of "doula" system in pregnancy provides a means of passing on special information

153

central to the community group. This approach is being used in Queensland, Australia to ensure that important "women's business" and traditional cultural practices associated with pregnancy and birth are passed on within the aboriginal community (Norbury 1996)

➡ Have your references available to support your statements. There will be some women who want to tackle entrenched routines and who need strong ammunition to arm their campaign. Others just want to be sure that they have all the resources available when considering their options. This could be especially relevant for a woman, who for example, is considering terminating a pregnancy if an abnormality is found during prenatal testing. When there are thorny emotional issues affecting a decision, wide reading can help crystallise values and beliefs. If you are unable to provide a buddy or support group for a woman, there may be written accounts that can fulfil some of the same needs.

Some women will also challenge your information, especially if it conflicts with what they have been told by others. If you have your references at hand, they will see that you are presenting a balanced picture, not just conjecture or personal opinion.

➡ Pay attention to the way you communicate — your language, expression, demeanour and interpretation. These issues were discussed in Chapter 3, and must be constantly borne in mind. They will also impact on her ability to make a decision, so be aware of any personal bias or preference that is colouring your information.

➡ Try to avoid overloading her with detail. In general, it is better to give her the basic skeleton with the opportunity to ask questions to flesh out the bones as she requires. Some women will want all the minute detail and others are happy with a broad sweep of good, basic information. There are others who deliberately avoid knowing too much, perhaps because they believe they really don't need to know or because they suspect they won't remember anyway. Let her be the judge of this, and use her further questions as a guide.

➡ Assume she already knows something. Very few adults will know nothing about pregnancy, birth or babies! If you take time to discover what she already knows, it can save you from wasting time on material with which she is already familiar. If, for example, you ask her "what have you heard about epidurals?" you may discover she knows the basics and just needs some specific details from you. This approach also lets you know just how informed a woman is about the care she is being offered. You may then have a duty to make sure she is given any missing facts, so that her decision is based on the whole story. This is an important point in making sure you have full consent for any medical procedures you may need to carry out.

Pre-natal classes

Most women attend pre-natal classes to obtain the information they need, especially if they don't have their "own" midwife to act as a personal guide. These classes are usually offered by hospitals and they are also sometimes available through community based groups such as The Childbirth Education Association, Parents Centres and The National Childbirth Trust. Usually they involve learning in groups with other expectant parents, with one or more leaders or educators teaching women and perhaps their partners about pregnancy and parenting issues.

Becoming involved in presenting pre-natal education is a natural extension of the midwifery role, yet one for which few midwives have adequate preparation. It is a responsible job, requiring skills in group leadership, educational methodology, specialised teaching strategies and an ability to use audiovisual teaching aids. Most midwives are "thrown in at the deep end", the apt title of a book on childbirth education (Handfield 1996), and left to sink or swim with little support for their new role. This is inexcusable, and completely unfair, for both the educator and the parents, who will likely have just this one opportunity for learning in this way before the baby comes.

Good education depends on the leaders of these groups having adequate training before undertaking this vital work. There are full training courses in most countries and smaller workshops are often available on specific topics or the development of practical teaching skills. There is a list of useful organisations who provide training courses listed in the appendix. General training in associated areas, such as basic counselling, group leadership skills, public speaking, assertiveness training, communication and conflict resolution also offer skills training useful for developing pre-natal class programs, and the personal and professional skills of midwives. If you are unable to attend a course, there are a number of books for childbirth educators that offer practical ideas and background information (Robertson 1994; Schott & Priest 1991; Wilson 1990; Hamer 1994; Bailey et al. 1992), and these are useful for those new to the field as well as those educators looking for new ideas for their classes.

It is often stated that the main purpose of pre-natal classes is to give parents the *information* they need about birth and parenting. Classes are often structured as a series of lectures, sometimes from a number of "experts", who tell parents what they believe they should know in order to do a good job. This approach has one major flaw: all the parents in the group are individuals who live in unique circumstances and who expect a baby with needs they cannot anticipate in advance. How can any "expert" know just what information these parents will ultimately need? Many assumptions are often made about the needs of parents and these are reflected in the content of the classes. In reality, no-one can know what the future will bring, and therefore what information parents may find useful.

A more realistic approach to pre-natal education is to place the emphasis on the acquisition and development of useful skills, rather than the absorption of facts. Pregnant women have a tendency to forget details (an effect of rising endorphin levels), yet they can learn and develop broad skills, especially if time for practice is incorporated into the program. What skills would new parents find useful?

- The ability to solve problems. This involves a number of steps, including gathering information, canvassing options, analysing choices, choosing and evaluating outcomes.
- Strategies for managing stress.
- Identifying and learning ways of using personal resources, including instincts and feelings.
- The ability to find and use resources within the community.
- Being able to identify personal limitations, strengths and weaknesses, including recognising crisis situations.
- Competency in basic communication as a foundation for the development of relationships, negotiation, and for resolving conflict.
- The ability to take responsibility.
- The capacity to be flexible.

Pre-natal programs that incorporate activities designed to build and strengthen these skills will enable prospective parents to feel better equipped to face any situation they may encounter. The acquisition of facts is less important in the pregnancy if parents know where and how they can find them if they have specific needs later. A lecture on calming a constantly crying baby seems academic, even a waste of time ("it won't be my baby who cries all night!") until the problem actually arises. If parents know where to find useful techniques at that point, the information becomes very relevant and practical. Most situations that are encountered by new parents fall into this category — a problem that needs a solution.

During the pregnancy and birth there will be many "problems" that pregnant women and their partners need to solve. Some may be minor, other may be very important, for example the decision to have an induction, or whether or not to have an amniocentesis. Each time parents are faced with a decision they have a chance to practise their skills, so that exercises undertaken as part of a pre-natal class are only one avenue for practice. In your role as a midwife, you will be an integral part of this problem solving for parents, perhaps as a resource person offering options they had not considered, perhaps as a sounding board as they consider their choices. Through your actions you can either reinforce their skills in this area (which is an empowering process for parents) or undermine them. Your role in pre-natal education, apart from the formal setting of a class, is vital in supporting parents and building their confidence. The more practice they have had before the baby arrives, the more confident they will be about the responsibilities of parenthood.

The format for classes and the kinds of activities that can be incorporated as skill building exercises is beyond the scope of this book. For a further exploration of these issues, see *Empowering Women — Teaching active birth in the 90s* (Robertson 1994). Such classes will be based on experiential learning, practical sessions, group involvement and discussion. There will be an emphasis on the needs of the individual learner and fulfilling their desired outcomes rather than covering a syllabus set by others. Opportunities for networking and learning from peers will be encouraged, and there will be provision for the exploration of feelings and emotions that colour many of the decisions parents make. Another important aspect will be examining cultures, beliefs and attitudes which have a significant influence on decision-making and the inclusion of the effects of the medical system on normal healthy pregnant women.

Pre-natal classes once focused on teaching women how to behave during labour and birth. "The breathing" was an integral part of each session, with women being taught how to consciously relax and shift their concentration away from their bodies. This approach was a good example of the medical culture prescribing a treatment for labour, with the ultimate goal of having a "painless" labour if the patient got it right. Like other aspects of medical care (such as the "selling" of epidurals, for example) it has become commercialised, with community groups offering services based around a product (such as psychoprophylaxis, "husband coached childbirth", Lamaze training, breath awareness, yoga and exercise). It is curious that this is the only natural bodily function to have been taken over in this way, and is perhaps a comment on the commercialisation and medicalisation of birth in a consumer-based society. Women do not need to be taught how to give birth or how to behave during labour any more than they need lessons in how to make love or behave during orgasm. These reproductive behaviours come naturally, driven by innate instincts present in all women. To suggest, and sell the idea, that women cannot give birth successfully without training is an insult to women and a denigration of their natural capacity for safe, effective birth. Training sessions based on learning specific techniques undermine a woman's confidence and set her up for failure if she forgets what to do or the method doesn't have the desired effect. This is profoundly disempowering for a new mother, at a time when she needs all the confidence and heightened feeling of self-esteem that she can muster.

There is a role for pre-natal classes in building skills, as we have seen, and in promoting a sense of community through networking and mutual experience between participants. A further benefit of working with parents in groups prenatally is the opportunity that arises for exploring the health care system and devising strategies for making it work for its clients in ways they have identified. A good example of this is the potential of early pregnancy groups, not only in bringing women and their partners together at a time when they are just coming to terms with the pregnancy, but also for examining the available choices in caregivers, birth places and medical surveillance techniques. Sessions in early pregnancy enable parents to fully explore these important issues that will have a direct impact on the kind of birth that eventuates. The most important decision a woman will make will be her choice of caregiver. If she is offered information about her options at 12 weeks of pregnancy it will be easier for her to shop around before making her decision. It can be more difficult to change caregivers later, since the system is geared to locking women into a specific stream of care as early as possible. Information is most relevant when people are making decisions. The potential for improving outcomes through provision of information early in the pregnancy is enormous, and one that should be made available to all women.

Many midwives find that offering pre-natal education through hospitals can be frustrating. The agenda of hospital-based classes is often one of presenting parents with the details of "what we do in our hospital" rather than ensuring that prospective parents are given the full facts and options concerning medical procedures. Thus sessions on pain relief may be given by an anaesthetist who talks primarily about epidurals while failing to mention the use of warm baths and massage to relieve pain; parents may be informed they will be monitored with a CTG for 30 minutes on admission without the explanation that this is a purely optional procedure; the giving of oxytocics for third stage and Vitamin K to the baby after birth pay be presented as hospital policy rather than choices available for the parents to consider. If educators fulfil their responsibility and offer a broader picture, including patients' rights and parents' choices, they may be threatened with sanctions and have their educational role curtailed. The legal issues surrounding these scenarios are discussed in Chapter 8. Educators often feel that they can offer better services for parents outside the hospital, as independent practitioners. This is worth considering, especially if you feel passionately about providing quality education for parents, however it does have its drawbacks. You will be in effect running a small (often very small) business, with all that this entails. You will have to make a charge for your classes, to cover your expenses and salary, and this may put the classes out of the reach of many parents who will continue to use the hospital classes, especially if they are free. However, you will probably find yourself working with a group of dedicated, motivated individuals, who, with the honing of their skills, are well placed to make changes within the system, for the ultimate benefit of the community as a whole. All the changes that have come about in maternity care have been consumer driven (rooming in, father at the birth, birth centres, revival of home birth options, unrestricted breast feeding, to name a few) and these parents learned about these issues within the community. Pre-natal classes can play a significant role in creating humanised birth options in hospitals, and as an educator, you can have a pivotal role in stimulating these changes. It is exciting and rewarding work.

Debriefing

Another valuable role for the midwife during a woman's pregnancy is enabling her to debrief her previous birth experiences. Many of the issues and outcomes of previous births come into sharp focus for a woman when she is pregnant with her next baby, and much unfinished business can surface. Until this is explored, and perhaps resolved, the woman may have mental blocks that restrict her ability to move forward through this next pregnancy. Taking time to examine her previous experiences may, in the end, make the following labour easier and faster, if emotional issues, fears, worries and anxieties have been dealt with in the pregnancy.

If you are seeing the woman throughout her entire pregnancy as her primary caregiver this discussion will be easy as you will have many occasions during which you can gently examine her past births. If you don't have the luxury of a caseload practice, then you will need to make opportunities for these discussions, perhaps even scheduling a specific time for them to be raised. You may be able to incorporate a discussion into the

- booking in session at the hospital: "Tell me how your last labour went?"
- labour ward tour: "Was this where you had your baby last time? What do you remember about the hospital last time you gave birth?"
- social events you share with her: "It is great you are pregnant again. Is there anything you want to differently this time?"
- phone conversations, when she calls the labour ward: "I wasn't here last time. How did that labour go?"
- clinic visit: "I see in your notes that you have had two babies already. How were their births?"

- post-natal reunion of the prenatal class group: "tell me how it all went. Was there anything that surprised you about the labour?"

Women generally love to talk about their births, and have a particular need to tell others when the labour was different from what they expected. Dramas, complications and unexpected events weigh heavily on women's minds and are part of a grieving process. Even if the birth went well, there can be disappointments and although if these may seem very minor, women need to be able to talk about them to someone. Disappointment and even grief are natural outcomes when expectations are not fulfilled, and women usually have some preconceived idea in their mind about how the birth will happen. Even if you have gone to great lengths to present the broad possibilities of birth in the hope that they will have an open mind to the possible outcomes, it seems that expectations form, and disappointment may result to some degree, if the birth turns out differently.

Your role in debriefing sessions can be very simple. You mainly need to listen, to reflect and clarify her feelings, acknowledge her reactions and then help her derive a positive outcome from the experience. Listening, reflecting and clarifying are basic tools for effective communication and have been discussed earlier. Facilitating the turning of a negative experience into a positive learning outcome is valuable for her personal growth, and one that you can initiate.

All of life's events offer chances to learn, and even in the face of great tragedy and disaster there are positives to be gained. Indeed, adversity can be a great stimulus for learning — we try not to make the same mistakes twice. Part of this learning process may involve having basic questions answered, to help her clarify exactly what transpired during a previous birth. If you were not present, you may be able to help her access her hospital records, or arrange for her to meet with the caregivers who were there. If you were at the birth, you may be able to relate the events from first hand experience, explaining what was done and why. You need to exercise care in doing this — to avoid implicating others or imparting a bias to your comments and to ensure an honest appraisal of what went on. You could suggest she speak to other carers at the birth, perhaps working with her to draw up a list of questions she could ask. It may be impossible to get all the answers, as many outcomes happen for unclear reasons, and you may need to find ways of enabling her to accept this fact, even if it is unsatisfactory from the point of view of resolving unfinished business. If her problems would appear to have the potential for having an overwhelming influence on the current pregnancy, it would be wise to refer her to someone who can provide specialised counselling, such as a bereavement counsellor (even if the baby didn't die), social worker, psychologist or other suitable therapist.

Labour ward tours

Another occasion during which you can offer valuable childbirth education is during the labour ward tour. Most women and their partners will visit the hospital to have at look at its facilities and to familiarise themselves with the area in which they will be labouring. This will probably be the only time that they will see the maternity unit before they arrive in labour. The impression they receive and the information they get on this visit will have a marked impact on their perception of what labour will be like. They will also form a view about what they will be "allowed" to do and gain an impression about the attitudes and practices of the staff who work there. This may also be the first time some women will have met a midwife, especially if their pre-natal care is carried out by a doctor and they were booked in by a clerk in administration. The opportunity presented by this contact with a midwife is profound, for both the woman and the caregiver.

Most parents will take part in this tour as part of a group. The leader may be the person who facilitated the pre-natal classes, or it may be led by one or more staff of the unit itself. Midwives often view the prospect of a mass of expectant parents tramping around the birth suite with alarm, and try to find an excuse to be somewhere else. This is a pity, since as a midwife you will have a captive audience of very receptive expectant parents hanging on every word you say! In addition, although you may not remember them individually, each woman is likely to remember you, which may be important if you are the only midwife she knows from the whole unit. Sighting you in labour could be very reassuring for her, and make it easier for her to settle into the unit in labour. So, how can you make the most of this visit?

➡ Recognise its potential for empowering the parents within the hospital setting. As you present details about the equipment, treatments, facilities, routines and procedures, make it plain that these are all available as services, should she wish to use them. Parents have the right to accept or reject anything offered to them, and this needs to be made clear. You will need to explain how they can ensure that their wishes are acted upon — show them how to use a birth plan, describe the procedure for having a note about their wishes recorded in their nursing notes and talk about ways of communicating their ideas to other staff.

➡ Tie the visit in with the pre-natal classes. Of course, you will need to have some idea of what has been happening in the classes before you can do this effectively. For example, invite the parents to try out the furniture and its suitability for making the woman comfortable in labour. Use chairs, mats and beanbags similar to those used for practice at the classes.

Show them where extra pillows are stored, where they can obtain a sheet to go over the beanbag, where the stacking chairs are located.

→ Encourage the parents to investigate the fittings and fixtures in the labour room itself. If one aim of the visit is familiarisation, then encouraging people to actually do something rather than just standing around looking is the best way of helping them to feel "at home". One way of doing this is to have a labour rehearsal, and create some scenarios: "Imagine she is saying that she feel she is going to be sick. See if you can find a suitable bowl for her". "Have a look for some extra towels — she wants to go and take a shower". "The pads she is using to catch the drips of amniotic fluid need changing. Where can you find some spares?" For some items, such as a bedpan, you will need to explain where the pan room can be found, and which ones are available to be used. You might also need to explain how the kitchen area works, and where drinks, ice blocks and light snacks can be obtained.

Some hospital staff take a dim view of adults wandering around "unsupervised" in their labour wards in this way, and this is a clear example of the lack of trust they have in people (and adults, in this case). If you want to empower people, and particularly labouring women, then their support people must be treated with respect and given responsibility. Considering them inferior, incapable or irresponsible is a form of discrimination, and apart from being insulting, is rude and unwelcoming. It may be that this adult who is being considered untrustworthy has a very responsible position at work — if they are out of their depth in this situation it is because they haven't been shown what to do. Avoid making unfair assumptions!

→ Explain how the system works, not as a way of gaining compliance ("this is what happens next … etc.") but as a means of helping them understand the procedure, so alternatives can be worked out if desired. You can also explain that different staff have different approaches to labour, and suggest ways of making their needs known to those who are less enthusiastic ("I am hoping to give birth to my baby kneeling on the floor. Can you help me with that?"). Show parents the notes that will be kept and tell them they can have their wishes recorded in them as a way of ensuring unauthorised procedures are not carried out without prior consultation.

→ Emphasise the normalcy of birth. Most labour rooms are cluttered with a number of pieces of technical equipment, all prominently displayed. This gives a clinical feel to the room which can be quite intimidating. Many tour leaders focus their attention on this equipment, proudly showing it off, and explain its workings in such detail that the impression is given that it is central to a successful outcome, and will therefore be used. The emphasis on technology can imply that complications are almost inevitable and that rescue procedures will almost certainly be needed. This can be frightening and create fear where none existed before. Many parents have come away from a labour ward tour very scared and worried, which completely negates the purpose of the visit.

A way of avoiding unintended anxiety is to down play the importance of the equipment in favour of a description of normal labour and the props and facilities available to support this process. If someone asks about one of the machines, or requests an explanation of a piece of equipment, you can speak directly to them, preferably semi-privately. If someone asks you a direct question, you have their permission to give an answer and provide information that they are actively seeking. If you gratuitously dump complex, technical and medical information on people who have not requested it, you are not only taking a risk that anxiety will be created, but you are taking a liberty. You have no right to alarm people, and though this is probably the last outcome you would wish, it can happen accidentally with surprising ease, given that you are dealing with sensitive adults in a very unfamiliar and somewhat threatening environment.

➡ One visit to the labour ward will probably not be enough to familiarise parents with the unit and its facilities. There is usually so much to see, all of it new and different, that it is impossible to absorb and understood it all in one short visit. One way around this is to offer supplementary visits, on a one-to-one basis, for parents who would like to know more. Hospitals are often too busy to accommodate these requests during the normal working week, but time may be found in the evening (which often suits working parents) or on weekends, when maternity units are often much quieter (fewer inductions and caesareans are scheduled for weekends).

In some hospitals, lending libraries are maintained for client use, and these are located in the maternity unit, so that on frequent visits to borrow and return books, contact can be made with the staff and the workings of the unit noted.

Other hospitals hold "open days", again often on a weekend, when the whole community is invited to "come and see where babies are born". Sometimes this is a regular event, on other occasions it may be part of a larger effort to throw open the whole hospital. These are often very popular events, and everyone likes to visit the maternity section. It provides a good opportunity for building communication links with the community, and greater insight into the needs and facilities of hospitals in general.

These are some ideas about extending the traditional notions of pre-natal education. All of them offer midwives ways of promoting midwifery and their own personal skills. In many communities, people are rather ignorant of what

163

midwives actually do, believing that they are a form of nurse, working for a doctor. Of course, in some cases they are right, yet much of the time this is a reflection of the general ignorance about midwifery. One very valuable form of pre-natal education is to take your message about birth and options in care to the community on a broad scale. Pre-natal education doesn't just have to focus on one woman and her special needs. It can take a global approach and involve mass education. Look for ways of spreading your message:

- displays in shopping malls
- speaking to community groups, especially those where young families gather
- writing articles for the local newspaper
- being interviewed by local radio or television stations
- leaflets in appropriate places: chemists, doctor's surgeries, family planning clinics etc.
- talking to school children
- career days in high schools
- joining professional groups in the community: Apex, Rotary, Lions etc.
- talking to friends and acquaintances about your work.

Every time you promote midwifery, you are creating awareness of options and choices for pregnant women to consider. People cannot choose a service they know nothing about, and you cannot practice your skills without women who want to have you at their births. In educating women about midwifery, you will also reap another benefit — learning more about birth and womens' needs. The learning need never stop, and that is what is so fascinating.

References

Bailey A., Hunter D. & Taylor B. 1992, *The Zen of Groups*, Tandem Press, New Zealand.

Hamer K. 1994, *Leading a Group*, Hamer Publications, Sydney, Australia.

Handfield B. 1996, *Thrown in at the deep end*, Handfield & Bell, Melbourne, Australia.

Norbury R. 1996, Clinical Nurse Consultant, Cairns Base Hospital, Cairns, Queensland, 4870. (personal communication).

Priest J. & Schott J. 1991, *Leading Antenatal Classes*, Butterwoth-Heinemann, UK.

Robertson A. 1994, *Empowering Women — teaching active birth in the 90s*, ACE Graphics, Sydney, Australia.

Wilson P. 1990, *Antenatal Teaching — A guide to Theory and Practice*, Faber, UK.

Chapter 10

MAKING IT HAPPEN

This book had described many ways in which you can expand and develop your skills and role as a midwife. We have looked at ways suggestions for improving communication with women, working with then during the pregnancy, supporting and assisting them during labour, acting as an advocate and encouraging the partner — all in an effort to offer the best midwifery services possible. Perhaps you are now thinking "How do I put all this into practice?".

There is no doubt it can be difficult. Routines, protocols and procedures are entrenched in many maternity units, and quite a few of your colleagues will be happy going on with things as they are and be unwilling to change. Hospital administrators are often reluctant to try something new, unless the current service is being heavily criticised by the community (which is rare, since women with new babies often have little time in which to complain). The medical fraternity are usually sitting comfortably, satisfied that the system has taken care of their particular needs, even if that has been achieved at the expense of others. Yet many midwives do feel dissatisfied and crave change, feeling an acute need to grow and develop professionally, not only to ensure women have more individualised births, but to fulfil their own personal objectives.

There have been many changes in maternity services over the past 10 years. Women are not now routinely separated from their babies at birth; fathers are welcome in the labour wards; women can move around and not be strapped to a bed during labour; there is recognition that women have unique needs during birth; and at last we are scientifically evaluating the safety and efficacy of the many treatments that have been imposed on labouring women and babies. The problem is that change is never fast enough. Change is also stressful and managing this requires skills, patience and resources, which are not always forthcoming. Since it is impossible to change the whole system yourself, how can you implement some changes for yourself and for the women with whom you will working?

The first step will be to gain confidence and insight into the wide variety of events and behaviours that are associated with normal birth. As discussed earlier, this may be difficult, or even impossible, to do if you work solely within a hospital maternity unit, so you will need to find other ways of expanding your experience:

➡ Find out what alternatives for birth exist in your community. Are there home births? Birth Centres? Community based midwifery services? Perhaps you could spend some time talking to the midwives who work in these areas, and discover how they approach their jobs. Visiting their clients and spending time in their units will enable you to see a variety of ways in which midwives can work.

➡ There are a number of books that examine alternative midwifery practices. Some of these books such as *Spiritual Midwifery*, first written in 1977 (Ina May Gaskin revised, 1990) and *Heart and Hands* (Davis 1987) are timeless classics, still very relevant for midwives today. Many modern texts have a rather clinical, sometimes scholarly approach to birth (even those on alternative therapies) and an emphasis on the technical aspects — very few have captured the essence of the process itself. Caroline Flint's *Sensitive Midwifery* is a notable exception (Flint 1986) in this regard.

➡ Attend conferences and study days which offer opportunities for sharing and discussing aspects of midwifery practice with which you may be unfamiliar. Interactive, participatory workshops offer more in this regard than conferences or didactic study days with limited scheduled opportunities for discussion.

➡ Talk to women who have had babies. Joining a new mothers' group in the community, such as La Leche League, The Nursing Mothers Association, The National Childbirth Trust, or Parents Centres New Zealand, will give you the chance to hear the views of consumers.

➡ Attend births as a support person. This is arguably the best way to learn about normal birth and womens responses. Friends may invite you to attend their births (being a midwife will make you particularly welcome) or you could offer your services as a support person in a more official capacity, perhaps through the hospital classes.

These general strategies may require you to commit time and effort. Remember that they form part of your on-going professional training, and are therefore worth including in your personal program for self-development.

Document the meetings you have attended, the visits you have made, the conferences and workshops in which you have participated. These records can all form part of your curriculum vitae.

As you explore these new avenues for learning about birth, keep a journal or diary of your discoveries. Make a note of women's behaviours and reactions, jot down the handy hints and strategies used by the midwives, record the physiological processes evident in the labours you are witnessing. A written record, especially one that also notes your own feelings and emotions, provides a basis for reflective evaluation at a later date. It is also tangible evidence of your growing experience, which is encouraging and exciting. You may even be able to add photographs to provide visual reference points and help cement your memories of the births you have seen.

Establish a revue process for yourself. If you begin by describing your professional goals and objectives, you will have a way of measuring your progress towards achieving them. These might include such statements as:

- I will arrange to witness a water birth.
- In the next 12 months I will attend 3 home births.
- I will establish a notebook for "handy hints" that promote physiological birth.
- I shall join the local breastfeeding mothers support group and attend 3 meetings in the next 6 months.
- In the next month, I will subscribe to a professional midwifery journal.
- I will arrange holidays now, to enable me to attend a particular midwifery conference.
- When I am in the nearest large city or overseas (on holiday) I will spend one day visiting their birth centre/independent midwifery practice/community based midwifery service.
- I will put aside one half day per month to spend in the University/Hospital/Midwifery School library researching questions I have compiled.
- Within the next month, I will join my local midwife support group.

Once you have prepared your goals, you can develop a plan to achieve these outcomes. As each one is accomplished, you will have a growing sense of satisfaction and achievement as you chart your professional development. Once you have completed all the tasks on your list, it will be time to prepare an extension to your program!

Apart from these broad goals, a set of steps to facilitate the revue of specific births can be helpful in identifying the special characteristics of the experience. Attending a birth with an open mind is a vital first step. If you approach the experience with the attitude that "this is just another labour" then you may miss notable details. Instead, try saying to yourself "I wonder what will be different about this birth? What will I see that will be new for me, as a midwife, and as a companion?". Since every woman labours in her own unique way, there will be new observations to make — you just want to be sure not to miss them. This approach will alert your sensitivity to the nuances of birth, and it will also make the event more interesting and stimulating. You will probably come away with questions ("I wonder why she did that, at that particular time?") and these can form the basis of your investigations in the library.

Later, talking about the birth with the woman and her partner will give you additional insights. No matter how you saw her labour, she will have a different version in her memory, and her partner will have his own perspective as well. Canvassing these impressions will give you more food for thought. Women are wonderful teachers for midwives, and they are so willing to share their ideas, that to miss out on these opportunities to learn from them would be a great pity.

Sharing birth stories with colleagues is also an important part of the process. Each of you will be seeing labours offering something different, and if you each share what you are observing, you will all gain experience more rapidly. There are several mechanisms for ensuring this sharing takes place:

➡ Regular staff meetings can be held in the maternity unit for the purpose of reviewing case histories. Additional reading or research could be presented to broaden the discussion. It is important to have a clear understanding of the purpose of these meetings: they can be used to review personal practice (as a form of peer review) but they could equally be used as a means of in-service education. Participants should know precisely on what basis they are being convened. It might be useful to extend an invitation to the doctors in your unit as well, since they are part of the team and could also benefit from examining birth in this way.

These staff meetings could also be used to review research articles, discuss broad professional issues, and formulate plans for action.

➡ Schedule informal gatherings, away from work, where stories, concerns and feelings can be aired. These may be regular events (once a month, say) or less frequent, according to need. Everyone benefits from a safe, supportive environment in which they can share emotions, especially about events that have happened to them in their professional lives. An empathetic listener, especially a colleague who understands the pressures and demands of the job, can create the atmosphere that is necessary for a frank exploration of personal feelings. This is particularly important when a disaster or tragedy has occurred and those involved need to debrief. These gatherings are also valuable for building a strong team approach to midwifery and this strength can be a powerful force for change within the unit and within the community as a whole. They will only be successful, however, if they take place in an atmosphere of love and acceptance, with no hint of recrimination or blame from colleagues.

➡ Another way of handling a crisis in a maternity unit is to have a formal process for involving counsellors or mediators (if appropriate) when these situations arise. Bringing someone in from outside, who was not involved directly in the event, acknowledges the serious nature of the crisis and the importance of resolving any personal issues that have arisen as a result. The effect of post traumatic shock syndrome on caregivers in other areas of medicine and in the community is well recognised and mechanisms are in place to provide the necessary support for firemen, ambulance officers and policemen, as well as for those in hospitals working in coronary care, intensive care, children's wards, palliative care etc. The need to extend this service to the maternity unit seems to have been overlooked, and yet this is one area where a death can be particularly devastating for staff (as well as for parents, of course) since it is not expected in a unit so focused on the creation of new life.

Many doctors and midwives carry painful memories of stillbirths and neonatal deaths in their hearts and minds for years, and sometimes these impact on personal and professional practices, even on occasion to the detriment of other labouring women. The wholesale application of electronic fetal monitors on all women in labour in an effort to forestall the occasional unavoidable intrapartum death is one example of the inappropriate use of technology — some babies will die during birth and no amount of fetal monitoring will save them. Unless the natural human reaction of wanting to avoid this terrible outcome through this kind of pro-active, but inappropriate, treatment is handled in a different way, many more women will be at risk of unnecessary intervention in an attempt to protect a caregiver's feelings. Hurt and grief are a part of life, to be accepted and dealt with, not ignored, avoided or glossed over.

➡ Formal support groups for midwives, such a professional organisations, play an important role in furthering collective needs and managing systemic change. A strong, dynamic representative group can be a powerful source of protection for midwives' rights and for the introduction of workplace reform, that will benefit not only its members, but ultimately pregnant women as well. Strong leadership is essential, and agreed aims and objectives must be negotiated so there is agreement on the group's role and function. These organisations can be national, but equally, they can be local, perhaps based around one regional area or even one particular hospital. Collective bargaining and lobbying are skills possessed by few midwives (or people generally), yet it only takes one person with these abilities to act as a spokesperson for a larger group for meaningful change to be precipitated. These leaders can only work effectively if they have good background support and the confidence and trust of the other group members. Since there is nothing like experience to build confidence, if such a leader is not immediately apparent in your group, if one or two people are prepared to "have a go", then with the assistance of the others, they may develop these valuable skills for the benefit of everyone.

Another way of gaining experience and broadening your knowledge of labour and birth is to undertake research. There will be many times, following a birth, when you will have questions for which answers may be hard to find. These could form the basis of a research project. Investigative projects don't necessarily have to be conducted as full randomised controlled trials, although this would be the appropriate approach in some instances. Research can also be done on a small scale, with good effect. For example, investigating the birth outcomes in your unit, or compiling personal practice results is a form of research. Disseminating your findings can have an impact on others and even change outcomes. In one hospital, a midwife compiled the details of episiotomy rates for each of the doctors who practised in her unit, and displayed the results in an anonymous bar chart on the wall in the unit. It was very apparent that one doctor had a very high rate of episiotomy compared to his colleagues, and as soon as this was evident (no names were attached to the chart) he realised how out of step he was, and altered his methods, no doubt to the relief of the midwives, and more importantly, to the women giving birth there.

If you do undertake a study, be sure to have your results published, whatever the finding, so that midwives elsewhere will be able to learn from your work. It is natural to want to publicise good findings; however, you should also pass on any adverse or disappointing results as well. Sometimes, knowing what does not work is just as useful as knowing what does, and it may save other midwives from using less than helpful techniques or management strategies in their work. There are various avenues for publishing your work: professional journals, midwives' newsletters, parents' magazines, newspapers and general magazines, chapters in a book, even writing your own book. Choose an appropriate medium that will best disseminate the type of information you have to share.

Being aware of what happens in your unit is an essential first step in initiating change. Take a look around, objectively, at the kinds of births that are occurring. How do they measure up to births in other hospitals? It might be worth visiting other maternity units and birth centres to learn how they approach birth — what can they show you that you could incorporate into your own personal practice, or initiate in your labour ward? It might save you much time and experimentation to take a leaf from another hospital's management manual, and strengthening your argument for providing a different service ("They are doing it successfully at ... hospital, and it has saved them money/ is very popular with the women/ has earned them good publicity" ... etc.).

If you decide that protocols need changing, a plan of action to achieve this needs to be developed. Usually a committee is invested with the task of reviewing practice standards for the unit. This group should comprise representatives of all the caregivers involved, including the midwives. They should meet regularly at advertised times and be open to the staff. If you wish to make a presentation to this committee, to pose a question ("Why are we doing ...?") or propose a change in the unit's protocols, you may need to take a number of steps:

➡ Obtain a list of committee members.

➡ Offer each one a copy of your proposal/presentation, and discuss any questions they may have.

➡ Have the item listed on the agenda. The group's secretary will take care of this.

➡ Offer to speak in support of your proposal. Be ready to answer questions, and have any additional documentation such as research articles on hand, with enough copies for group members.

➡ If the issue is complex, or sensitive, request time for group members to consider your points, perhaps having it listed for further discussion at a future meeting. Rushed decisions may go against you.

➡ Lobby committee members further, in the interim, to answer questions, provide additional information and encourage them to consider the wider implications.

➡ If there is reluctance to institute a permanent change, suggest an appropriate trial period, and offer staff training and an evaluation process to defuse argument and demonstrate your commitment.

➡ Publicise the outcome (whatever it is) to your colleagues and perhaps to the women, if this is appropriate. Include the committee's reasons for its decision and make copies of your proposal available publicly. It is important that everyone concerned knows what is happening, and on what grounds further action may be required (the evaluation, for example, or a further submission if you were unsuccessful).

Sometimes, a reverse approach can be used. Instead of approaching the committee with a proposal for change, request that they provide you with the reasoned justification for the protocols already in place. All protocol statements should include the research evidence and literature references on which they are based: requests for this information are quite justified on professional

171

grounds, especially if hospital administrators and staff are concerned about potential legal challenges.

Perhaps you are happy with the protocols, but feel that you could be offering new or extended services. Can you produce evidence that they are needed/wanted/supported by the community? A survey could provide you with these answers, and you can canvass women and their partners in various ways:

- hand out questionnaires in the post natal ward (part of the audit process),
- use postal surveys as a follow up several months after the birth,
- have questionnaires completed at booking in ("What kind of service would you like to have...?"),
- talking to parents through community groups,
- have surveys completed by the general public, in shopping centres, for example,
- use phone in/talk back programs on local radio stations.

Once you have your data, you can prepare a submission for presentation to your unit manager, the hospital administration or the hospital board, as appropriate. You will need to garner the support of your colleagues to help you prepare your submission. Presenting it as a team effort also shows you have the good will of your peers. You may need to lobby members of hospital committees, and to make a verbal presentation at any meetings when your plans are to be discussed. Rallying members of the public may also lend weight to your proposal, and this support could come in the form of letters, petitions or even personal representation to the various committee members.

One argument often given for retaining the status quo is that staffing levels won't permit better midwifery services, especially if the plan for improvement includes a proposal for more continuity of care by midwives, which is viewed by administrators as costly. This is a spurious argument, since there are a number of studies cited in The Cochrane Collaboration that demonstrate the cost-effectiveness of midwifery, particularly when on-going gains such as improved rates of breastfeeding and lower rates of admission to hospital by babies in their first year are taken into account. There is abundant evidence that midwifery care leads to improved birth outcomes which translates into fewer days in hospital post partum for women. During your visit to the library, assemble this data and append it to your proposal. A trial period of six or twelve months could be suggested as a means of evaluating the costs involved for your particular unit, and this close scrutiny will also expose the real costs of medical alternatives. A healthier mother and baby must cost the health system less in terms of real dollars, quite apart from the wider benefits to the community in lower taxes, healthier populations and improved family life.

Money may also be saved if the current zeal for buying the latest equipment is tempered. Fancy hydraulic beds may help "sell" the hospital as progressive, but do they really add much to the quality of a woman's labour? The partner may enjoy pushing the buttons, while the woman may find labour more comfortable on a floor mat. Does the hospital really need to buy the latest in electronic fetal monitoring machines? Now that the scientific evidence has clearly exposed this technology as worthless for low risk women, and expensive, in terms of creating more caesareans and forceps deliveries, perhaps it can be sidelined in favour of appointing an extra midwife to the staff.

A closely related issue is the chronic under staffing of maternity units and the consequence of overworked midwives who have little enough time to fulfil their current duties, quite apart from the attention they would like to be able to give the women in their care. Time management is an important issue for us all, and we need to be constantly seeking ways of better using the time we do have available. Possible solutions for midwives might include:

➡ Careful assessment of your job description to see if there are any tasks you are doing that can, or should, be done by someone else. For example, some of the paperwork might be just as efficiently carried out by a clerk or midwifery assistant (who will be on a lower salary). Are you performing medical procedures for private patients that should rightly be done by the doctor? Are you cleaning up after student doctors or midwives, when this should be part of their learning?

➡ Admitting fewer women for inductions, except in case of provable medical necessity. Supervising a women who is being induced takes time and considerable attention, especially if she needs an epidural or other flow-on interventions. Watching monitors, attending to infusions, siting drips, charting blood pressures etc. are nursing procedures, which might be just as efficiently carried out by others, leaving midwives available to exercise their professional skills more effectively with other women. This is a radical thought, but one worth considering!

If a doctor or anaesthetist is encouraging women to use more epidurals then they should also be pushing administrators for the extra staff required for safely monitoring their effects. Alternatively, if no extra staff will be available, then midwives might consider lobbying the doctors to order fewer drugs and anaesthetics, since safety cannot be guaranteed without supervision, and the doctor and hospital may be challenged legally if they ordered a procedure knowing that there are insufficient staff to supervise it safely.

173

➡ Re-assessment of the paperwork required of midwives. The advent of computers should have made recording the details easier, but many midwives waste valuable time mastering the foibles of computers. A training course in computer skills for all staff might save time and energy in the long run, and standardisation of all computer programs in hospitals would reduce the stress on new staff who have to learn a completely different system with each new appointment. Streamlining the paperwork would be a good staff project for unit meetings, and provide a popular common purpose that would not only have the potential for improving working conditions, but promote unit cohesiveness as it is undertaken.

If fund raising will be needed (very likely with current shortfalls in health budgets), investigate potential funding sources within the community. Service clubs, women's groups, parents' groups and government departments may all be prepared to support your plan and offer financial assistance. Many changes can be brought about in maternity services without the need to spend money at all, and others, such as redecorating, may attract sponsorship from local businesses. Major renovations, such as changing the plumbing to install a bath, will require capital expenditure, which may not be available from general hospital revenues. Your ingenuity may be tested, but one advantage of seeking community support is the automatic publicity you will generate, both for midwifery and for the progressive approach of the hospital. There are many opportunities for advertising your new services, such as:

- an official opening of new facilities,
- an article on "the first baby born in the new waterbirth pool" in the local newspaper,
- interior photographs of the redecorated labour rooms in the maternity unit information leaflet given to women when they book in,
- an open day to view the extended/new facilities,
- listing the donations in the newspaper,
- honouring corporate sponsorships with a plaque on the wall or on the equipment,
- a photographic display in the shopping centre on International Midwives' Day,
- giving interviews on the local radio and television.

Changing your personal practice

Trying out the ideas in this book may present some personal challenges. Firstly there will be the normal discomfort that arises from attempting anything with which you are unfamiliar — the learning curve may be steep at first. It may help to remember that once you were totally unfamiliar with all aspects of midwifery practice (can you remember how that felt?) and yet you were able, with time and effort, to incorporate the techniques into your daily professional activities. You are probably so familiar with them now that you perform many tasks without even thinking. Learning something new always involves taking risks at the beginning. Initially, there is accepting that current strategies may need updating (this can be uncomfortable enough) and then there is the awkwardness that stems from unfamiliarity with the new ways. With practise, the new skills develop and grow, to finally become as comfortable and familiar as the old ways. At least you have one enormous advantage from trying something new at this point in your career: you are already a midwife, childbirth educator or labour support person, and therefore you are not trying to learn everything at once, as you needed to do when you were a student. Your current experience will enable you to experiment with changing some parts of your practice, whilst still feeling competent overall.

When you are trying out some of these new ideas, offer them to the multiparous women with whom you are working. They too have experience, and they are therefore more willing to try something different, especially if it means an improvement on what happened before. These women generally have shorter labours, so the results can be assessed sooner. This is very useful when you are educating your colleagues — they may be able to see the birth through to its conclusion (and assess for themselves the effects of your ideas) before they leave at the end of their shift.

A second challenge might come from your colleagues, who feel threatened and wary, particularly if they are basically unwilling to change and incorporate new ideas. The easiest way to educate them about the new approach is to show them how it is done. Seeing it for themselves is a clear demonstration of how it can be done, and this is much more effective than just telling them about it. Once they see how to apply hot wet towels to relieve back pain in labour, for example, and hear the ecstatic response from the woman, they will not need convincing that this is a marvellous alternative for relieving pain. The next step will be for them to try it themselves, and, as they experiment, you can support their efforts. Positive feedback, from both you and from the woman in labour, goes a long way towards convincing doubting colleagues that they too, can try new ideas with success. Avoid criticism as this is discouraging and undermines confidence. Professional practitioners like to feel their status and position are not being threatened, especially while they are learning, so find ways of nurturing them as they assimilate the new ideas. This is especially important when educating doctors, who are often very reluctant to try new ideas, particularly those which seem more related more to midwifery than medicine.

One final step in trying out these ideas is to constantly review your results. You won't always get it right, some suggestions may not work as well as you hoped and occasionally you will make mistakes. These outcomes, although at times regrettable and painful, are important signposts on the road to learning. They will pull you up, make you question and force you to think again. Without them we would lose the stimulus for change and our lives would lack the richness and variety that stems from innovation.

You are lucky to be working in a field that is infinitely rewarding, constantly challenging and full of potential excitement. Make the most of it!

References

Davis E. 1989, *Heart and Hands: A midwife's guide to pregnancy and birth*, Celestial Arts, California, USA.

Flint C. 1986, *Sensitive Midwifery*, Heinemann, London, UK.

Gaskin I. 1990, *Spiritual Midwifery*, The Book Publishing Company, Tennessee, USA.

APPENDIX

Sources of books and teaching aids

ACE Graphics (Australia)

PO Box 366
Camperdown NSW 2050
Australia
Phone: +61 (0)2 9660 5177
Fax: +61 (0)2 9660 5147

ACE Graphics (United Kingdom)

PO Box 173
Sevenoaks Kent
United Kingdom TN14 5ZT
Phone: +44 (0)1959 524 622
Fax: +44 (0)1959 524 622

Childbirth Graphics

PO Box 21207
Waco Texas
USA 76702-9964
Phone: +1 800 299 3366 (within USA)
Fax: +1 817 751 0221

ICEA Bookcenter

PO Box 20048
Minneapolis Minnesota
USA 55420
Phone: +1 800 624 4934 (within USA)
Fax: +1 612 854 8772

Emily's Store

5430 Lynx Lane #139
Columbia Maryland
USA 21044
Phone: +1 800 757 6166 (within USA)
Fax: +1 410 740 9260

MIDIRS

9 Elmdale Road
Clifton, Bristol
United Kingdom BS8 1SL
Phone: 0800 58 1009 (within the UK)
Fax: +44 (0)117 925 1792

Organisations that offer training for childbirth educators

Associates in Childbirth Education

PO Box 366
Camperdown NSW
Australia 2050
Phone: +61 (0)2 9660 5177
Fax: +61 (0)2 9660 5147

International Childbirth Education Association

Box 20048
Minneapolis Minnesota
USA 55420
Phone: +1 800 624 4934 (within USA)
Fax: +1 612 854 8772

National Childbirth Trust

Alexandra House
Oldham Terrace
Acton, London
United Kingdom W3 6NH
Phone: +44 (0)181 992 8637
Fax: +44 (0)181 992 5929

Parents Centre New Zealand

PO Box 17-351
Wellington
New Zealand
Phone: +64 (0)4 476 6950
Fax: +64 (0)4 476 6949

INDEX

A

aboriginal health 154
active management of labour 15
adrenalin 50–53, 54–55, 58, 107
    effects 52
    impact on endorphin levels 51
    symptoms 50
advocacy
    direct action 145
    during labour 136
    for colleagues 140
aromatherapy 82
augmentation 108
Australia 14, 142
autonomy 33, 34, 36, 71, 121

B

birth
    basic truths 9
    beliefs and attitudes 28
    culture 125
    medicalisation of 6, 9
    physiology 39–55
    see also labour
birth plans 17, 23, 122, 138, 147
bonding 49
breastfeeding 105, 115

C

catecholamines, see adrenalin
Childbirth Education Association 155
The Cochrane Collaboration 114, 138, 172
comfort in labour 75–86
communication 144, 154
    bias 22
    feedback 23
    language 12, 19–24
    non-verbal 21, 29
    skills 29, 141
complications during birth 106–115, 107, 110
consent 137, 155

D

debriefing 125, 141, 145, 159–160, 168
dependency 33, 93
double standards 12
doula 27
due date 58

E

endorphins 44–49, 57, 58, 108, 110
    assessing levels 48
    effects of 45
    signs of 62
    third day blues 49
epidural anaesthetics 52, 111–112, 173
evidence based practice 7

F

fathers 120, 123–125, 133, 148
Federal Food and Drug Administration 14
Ferguson's Reflex 40
fetal distress 42, 94
fetal monitoring 109–110
fetus ejection reflex 53
first stage of labour 46, 60, 63

G

goody bag
    for labour 70
    for siblings 129

H

Having a Baby in Europe 6
hospital
    admission procedures 35, 68
    ground rules 34
    private patients 16
    protocols and procedures 7, 14, 26, 36, 126, 137, 165, 171, 172
    standing orders 15

I

induction 58, 59, 61, 108, 173
informed choice 14, 16, 131, 133–135
    concept of 134
    right to 134, 135
informed consent 142
    see also consent
initiating change 165
    see also advocacy
instincts 39
interventions, see obstetric interventions

K

keeping women off the bed 77, 147

L

La Leche League 166
labour
    after the baby is born 104–106
    anterior lip of cervix 47
    failure to progress 51, 52, 107
    going to hospital 67
    posterior position 42, 84
    see also birth
labour ward tours 34, 121, 161–163
Lamaze 157
legal issues 14, 140–145
    informed consent 15, 142
    reducing vulnerability 144
legislation 143

M

Marsden Wagner 143
massage 82–84
maternal exhaustion 95
medical model 8, 12, 17, 28, 131, 133
meperidine 112
Michel Odent 11
midwife
    aims and objectives 9, 167
    as an advocate 131, 132
    changing personal practice 174
    evaluation 176
    responsibilities 16, 140, 141
    role of 5–10, 124, 135, 137, 139, 141, 159, 165
    support 168
    training 5, 7, 17, 25
midwifery 172
    education of colleagues 175
    experience 166, 170
    medications, giving of 13
    professional organisations 169
    promotion 122, 163, 164, 174
    system 150, 151
    time management 173
    training 145
music 82

N

The National Childbirth Trust 155, 166
The Netherlands 14, 16
New Zealand 14, 16, 166
Niles Newton 43, 53
nitrous oxide 112
nocebo effect 11, 72
nor-adrenalin 50, 54
    see also adrenalin
The Nursing Mothers Association 166

O

observations 71–75
    fetal heart tones 73
    internal examinations 22, 73, 86
    palpation 73

obstetric interventions 12, 106, 107, 114–115, 137, 147
    see also complications
oxytocin 40, 40–44, 60
    inhibition 43
    nipple stimulation 43
    result of stimulation 40
    results of 44
    stimulating 43

P

pain in labour 45–49
    causes of 47
    need for 45
    psychological advantages 46
    sources of 46
pain relief 14, 81–84
    epidural 52, 111–112, 173
    hot packs 81
    pelvic rocking 86
panic behaviours 31–33
    signs of 32
Parents Centres 155, 166
pelvic floor muscles 42, 47, 96
pelvis, role in labour 53
perineum 42, 47
    protecting 101
pethidine 112
positions
    comfort check list 76
    going to hospital 68
    of the midwife 72
    second stage 98–101
    see also comfort in labour
pre-natal classes 120, 149–164
    aims and objectives 152
    early pregnancy 158
    format of 157
    giving information 153–155
    labour rehearsal 121
    opportunities for education 151
    skills for parents 156
problem solving 34, 134, 156

R

rapport 29, 30, 62, 141
    achieving 22, 28, 29
    personality clashes 31
    with women in a panic 32
research 17, 170, 171
    using 141, 144, 154
resources 177–178
rupture of membranes 42, 61, 110

S

second stage of labour 47, 92–104
self help
    in first stage 60
    in second stage 95–98
    last weeks of pregnancy 58
    positions in first stage 64
    see also comfort in labour, positions
sexual abuse 36
siblings 61, 127–129
social model 8, 28
support
    during labour 26, 122
    during pregnancy 120
    emotional assistance 26
    providing 26
    "rescues" 27
    see also comfort in labour, positions
support people 34, 61, 64, 69, 70, 115, 117–129
    choosing 118–119, 126
    strategies for assisting 122, 124, 126
    uninvited guests 125
Sydney 23

T

TENS 114
The Social Meaning of Midwifery 6, 26
third stage of labour 104
training courses 155
    see also resources
transition 42, 48, 54, 86–92, 139

U

unexpected outcomes 160, 169
United Kingdom 13, 16, 142, 143
United States 14, 27, 142, 143

W

water, using 87–92
    bath 32, 54, 89, 107, 111, 112, 124
    general precautions 92
    hot towels 91
    pool 89
    shower 32, 90, 108, 111, 112, 124
witch hunt 143
World Health Organisation 6